THE LONDON AND BREWER

Anonymous

1736

THE PREFACE.

The many Inhabitants of Cities and Towns, as well as Travellers, that have for a long time suffered great Prejudices from unwholsome and unpleasant Beers and Ales, by the badness of Malts, underboiling the Worts, mixing injurious Ingredients, the unskilfulness of the Brewer, and the great Expense that Families have been at in buying them clogg'd with a heavy Excise, has moved me to undertake the writing of this Treatise on Brewing, Wherein I have endeavour'd to set in sight the many advantages of Body and Purse that may arise from a due Knowledge and Management in Brewing Malt Liquors, which are of the greatest Importance, as they are in a considerable degree our Nourishment and the common Diluters of our Food; so that on their goodness depends very much the Health and Longevity of the Body.

This bad Economy in Brewing has brought on such a Disrepute, and made our Malt Liquors in general so odious, that many have been constrain'd, either to be at an Expence for better Drinks than their Pockets could afford, or take up with a Toast and Water to avoid the too justly apprehended ill Consequences of Drinking such Ales and Beers.

Wherefore I have given an Account of Brewing Beers and Ales after several Methods; and also several curious Receipts for feeding, fining and preserving Malt Liquors, that are most of them wholsomer than the Malt itself, and so cheap that none can object against the Charge, which I thought was the ready way to supplant the use of those unwholsome Ingredients that have been made too free with by some ill principled People meerly for their own Profit, tho' at the Expence of the Drinker's Health.

_I hope I have adjusted that long wanted Method of giving a due Standard both to the Hop and Wort, which never was yet (as I know of) rightly ascertain'd in Print before, tho' the want of it I am perswaded has been partly the occasion of the scarcity of good Drinks, as is at this time very evident in most Places in the Nation. I have here also divulg'd the Nostrum of the Artist Brewer that he has so long valued himself upon, in making a right Judgment when the Worts are boiled to a true Crisis; a matter of considerable Consequence, because all strong Worts may be boiled too much or too little to the great Loss of the Owner, and without this Knowledge a Brewer must go on by Guess; which is a hazard that every one ought to be free from that can; and therefore I have endeavor'd to explode the old Hour-glass way of Brewing, by reason of the several Uncertainties that attend such Methods and the hazard of spoiling both Malt and Drink; for in short where a Brewing is perform'd by Ladings over of scalding Water, there is no occasion for the Watch or Hour-glass to boil the Wort by, which is best known by the Eye, as I have both in this and my second Book made appear.

I have here observed that necessary Caution, which is perfectly requisite in the

Choice of good and the Management of bad Waters; a Matter of high Importance, as the Use of this Vehicle is unavoidable in Brewing, and therefore requires a strict Inspection into its Nature; and this I have been the more particular in, because I am sensible of the great Quantities of unwholsome Waters used not only by Necessity, but by a mistaken Choice.

So also I have confuted the old received Opinion lately published by an Eminent Hand, that long Mashings are the best Methods in Brewing; an Error of dangerous Consequence to all those who brew by Ladings over of the hot Water on the Malt.

The great Difficulty and what has hitherto proved an Impediment and Discouragement to many from Brewing their own Drinks, I think, I have in some measure removed, and made it plainly appear how a Quantity of Malt Liquor may be Brewed in a little Room and in the hottest Weather, without the least Damage by Foxing or other Taint.

The Benefit of Brewing entire Guile small Beer from fresh Malt, and the ill Effects of that made from Goods after strong Beer or Ale; I have here exposed, for the sake of the Health and Pleasure of those that may easily prove their advantage by drinking of the former and refusing the latter.

By the time the following Treatise is read over and thoroughly considered, I doubt not but an ordinary Capacity will be in some degree a better Judge of good and bad Malt Liquors as a Drinker, and have such a Knowledge in Brewing that formerly he was a stranger to; and therefore I am in great Hopes these my Efforts will be one Principal Cause of the reforming our Malt Liquors in most Places; and that more private Families than ever will come into the delightful and profitable Practice of Brewing their own Drinks, and thereby not only save almost half in half of Expence, but enjoy such as has passed thro' its regular Digestions, and is truly pleasant, fine, strong and healthful.

I Question not but this Book will meet with some Scepticks, who being neither prejudiced against the Introduction of new Improvements, or that their Interests will be hereby eclipsed in time; To such I say I do not write, because I have little hopes to reform a wrong Practice in them by Reason and Argument. But those who are above Prejudice may easily judge of the great Benefits that will accrue by the following Methods, I have here plainly made known, and of those in my Second Book that I have almost finished and hope to publish in a little time, wherein I shall set forth how to Brew without boiling Water or Wort, and several other Ways that will be of considerable Service to the World_.

4

CHAP. I.

Of the Nature of the Barley-Corn, and of the proper Soils and Manures for the Improvement thereof.

This Grain is well known to excel all others for making of Malts that produce those fine *British* Liquors, Beer and Ale, which no other Nation can equalize; But as this Excellency cannot be obtain'd unless the several Ingredients are in a perfect State and Order, and these also attended with a right judgment; I shall here endeavour to treat on their several particulars, and first of Soils.

This Grain I annually sow in my Fields on diversities of Soils, and thereby have brought to my knowledge several differences arising therefrom. On our Red Clays this Grain generally comes off reddish at both ends, and sometimes all over, with a thick skin and tuff nature, somewhat like the Soil it grows in, and therefore not so valuable as that of contrary qualities, nor are the black blewish Marly Clays of the Vale much better, but Loams are, and Gravels better than them, as all the Chalks are better then Gravels; on these two last Soils the Barley acquires a whitish Body, a thin skin, a short plump kernel, and a (unreadable) flower, which occasions those, fine pale and amber Malts made at *Dunstable*, *Tring* and *Dagnal* from the Barley that comes off the white and gravelly Grounds about those Places; for it is certain there is as much difference in Barley as in Wheat or other Grain, from the sort it comes off, as appears by the excellent Wheats that grow in the marly vale Earths, Peas in Sands, and Barley in Gravels and Chalks, &c. For our Mother Earth, as it is destined to the service of Man in the production of Vegetables, is composed of various sorts of Soils for different Seeds to grow therein. And since Providence has been pleased to allow Man this great privilege for the imployment of his skill and labour to improve the same to his advantage; it certainly behoves us to acquaint ourselves with its several natures, and how to adapt an agreeable Grain and Manure to their natural Soil, as being the very foundation of enjoying good and bad Malts. This is obvious by parallel Deductions from Turneps sown on rank claycy loamy Grounds, dressed with noxious Dungs that render them bitter, tuff, and nauseous, while those that grow on Gravels, Sands and Chalky Loams under the assistance of the Fold, or Soot, Lime, Ashes, Hornshavings, &c. are sweet (unreadable) and pleasant. 'Tis the same also with salads, Asparagus, Cabbages, Garden-beans and all other culinary Ware, that come off those rich Grounds glutted with the great quantities of *London* and other rank Dungs which are not near so pure, sweet and wholsome, as those produced from Virgin mould and other healthy Earths and Manures.

There is likewise another reason that has brought a disreputation on some of the Chiltern-barley, and that is, the too often sowing of one and the same piece of Ground, whereby its spirituous, nitrous and sulphureous qualities are exhausted and worn out, by the constant attraction of its best juices for the nutriment of the

Grain: To supply which, great quantities of Dungs are often incorporated with such Earths, whereby they become impregnated with four, adulterated, unwholsome qualities, that so affect the Barley that grows therein, as to render it incapable of making such pure and sweet Malts, as that which is sown in the open Champaign-fields, whose Earths are constantly rested every third Year called the Fallow-season, in order to discharge their crude, phlegmatick and sour property, by the several turnings that the Plough gives them part of a Winter and one whole Summer, which exposes the rough, clotty loose parts of the Ground, and by degrees brings them into a condition of making a lodgment of those saline benefits that arise from the Earths, and afterwards fall down, and redound so much to the benefit of all Vegetables that grow therein, as being the essence and spring of Life to all things that have root, and tho' they are first exhaled by the Sun in vapour from the Earth as the spirit or breath thereof, yet is it return'd again in Snows, Hails, Dews, etc. more than in Rains, by which the surface of the Globe is saturated; from whence it reascends in the juices of Vegetables, and enters into all those productions as food, and nourishment, which the Creation supplies.

Here then may appear the excellency of steeping Seed-barley in a liquor lately invented, that impregnates and loads it with Nitre and other Salts that are the nearest of all others to the true and original Spirit or Salt of the Earth, and therefore in a great measure supplies the want thereof both in inclosure and open Field; for even in this last it is sometimes very scarce, and in but small quantities, especially after a hot dry Summer and mild Winter, when little or no Snows have fell to cover the Earth and keep this Spirit in; by which and great Frosts it is often much encreased and then shews itself in the warmth of well Waters, that are often seen to wreak in the cold Seasons. Now since all Vegetables more or less partake of those qualities that the Soil and Manures abound with in which they grow; I therefore infer that all Barley so imbibed, improves its productions by the ascension of those saline spirituous particles that are thus lodged in the Seed when put into the Ground, and are part of the nourishment the After-Crop enjoys; and for this reason I doubt not, but when time has got the ascendant of prejudice, the whole Nation will come into the practice of the invaluable Receipt published in two Books, entituled, *Chiltern and Vale Farming Explained*, and, *The Practical Farmer*; both writ by *William Ellis* of *Little Gaddesden* near *Hempstead* in *Hertfordshire*, not only for Barley, but other Grains.

But notwithstanding Barley may grow on a light Soil with a proper Manure; and improved by the liquor of this Receipt, yet this Grain may be damaged or spoiled by being mown too soon, which may afterwards be discovered by its shrivelled and lean body that never will make right good Malt; or if it is mown at a proper time, and if it be housed damp, or wettish, it will be apt to heat and mow-burn, and then it will never make so good Malt, because it will not spire, nor come so regularly on the floor as that which was inned dry.

Again, I have known one part of a Barley-crop almost green at Harvest, another part ripe, and another part between both, tho' it was all sown at once, occasion'd by the several situations of the Seed in the Ground, and the succeeding Droughts. The deepest came up strong and was ripe soonest, the next succeeded; but the uppermost, for want of Rain and Cover, some of it grew not at all, and the rest was green at Harvest. Now these irregularities are greatly prevented and cured by the application of the ingredients mentioned in the Receipt, which infuses such a moisture into the body of the Seed, as with the help of a little Rain and the many Dews, makes it spire, take root and grow, when others are ruined for want of the assistance of such steeping.

Barley like other Grain will also degenerate, and become rank, lean and small bodied, if the same Seed is sown too often in the Soil; 'tis therefore that the best Farmers not only change the Seed every time, but take due care to have it off a contrary Soil that they sow it in to; this makes several in my neighbourhood every Year buy their Barley-seed in the Vale of *Ailsbury*, that grew there on the black clayey marly Loams, to sow in Chalks, Gravels, &c. Others every second Year will go from hence to *Fullham* and buy the Forward or Rath-ripe Barley that grows there on Sandy-ground; both which Methods are great Improvements of this Corn, and whether it be for sowing or malting, the plump, weighty and white Barley- corn, is in all respects much kinder than the lean flinty Sorts.

CHAP. II

Of making Malts.

As I have described the Ground that returns the best Barley, I now come to treat of making it into Malt; to do which, the Barley is put into a leaden or tyled Cistern that holds five, ten or more Quarters, that is covered with water four or six Inches above the Barley to allow for its Swell; here it lyes five or six Tides as the Malster calls it, reckoning twelve Hours to the Tide, according as the Barley is in body or in dryness; for that which comes off Clays, or has been wash'd and damag'd by Rains, requires less time than the dryer Grain that was inned well and grew on Gravels or Chalks; the smooth plump Corn imbibing the water more kindly, when the lean and steely Barley will not so naturally; but to know when it is enough, is to take a Corn end-ways between the Fingers and gently crush it, and if it is in all parts mellow, and the husk opens or starts a little from the body of the Corn, then it is enough: The nicety of this is a material Point; for if it is infus'd too much, the sweetness of the Malt will be greatly taken off, and yield the less Spirit, and so will cause deadness and sourness in Ale or Beer in a short time, for the goodness of the Malt contributes much to the preservation of all Ales and Beers. Then the water must be drain'd from it very well, and it will come equal and better on the floor, which may be done in twelve or sixteen Hours in temperate weather, but in cold, near thirty. From the Cistern it is put into a square Hutch or Couch, where it must lye thirty Hours for the Officer to take his Gage, who allows four Bushels in the Score for the Swell in this or the Cistern, then it must be work'd Night and Day in one or two Heaps as the weather is cold or hot, and turn'd every four, six or eight Hours, the outward part inwards and the bottom upwards, always keeping a clear floor that the Corn that lies next to it be not chill'd; and as soon as it begins to come or spire, then turn it every three, four or five Hours, as was done before according to the temper of the Air, which greatly governs this management, and as it comes or works more, so must the Heap be spreaded and thinned larger to cool it. Thus it may lye and be work'd on the floor in several parallels, two or three Foot thick, ten or more Foot broad, and fourteen or more in length to Chip and Spire; but not too much nor too soft; and when it is come enough, it is to be turned twelve or sixteen times in twenty-four Hours, if the Season is warm, as in *March, April* or *May*; and when it is fixed and the Root begins to be dead, then it must be thickned again and carefully kept often turned and work'd, that the growing of the Root may not revive, and this is better done with the Shoes off than on; and here the Workman's Art and Diligence in particular is tryed in keeping the floor clear and turning the Malt often, that it neither moulds nor Aker-spires, that is, that the Blade does not grow out at the opposite end of the Root; for if it does, the flower and strength of the Malt is gone, and nothing left behind but the Aker-spire, Husk and Tail: Now when it is at this degree and fit for the Kiln, it is often practised to put it into a Heap and let it lye twelve Hours before it is turned, to heat and mellow, which will much improve the Malt if it is done with moderation, and after that time it must be turned every six Hours during twenty four; but if it is overheated, it will become like Grease and be spoiled, or at least cause the Drink to be unwholsome; when this Operation is over, it then must be put on the Kiln to dry four, six or twelve Hours, according to the nature of the Malt, for the pale sort requires more leisure and less fire than the amber or brown sorts: Three Inches thick was formerly thought a sufficient depth for the Malt to lye on the Hair-cloth, but now six is often allowed it to a fault; fourteen or sixteen Foot square will dry about two Quarters if the Malt lyes four Inches thick, and here it should be turned every two, three or four Hours keeping the Hair-cloth clear: The time of preparing it from the Cistern to the Kiln is uncertain; according to the Season of the Year; in moderate weather three Weeks is often sufficient. If the Exciseman takes his Gage on the floor he allows ten in the Score, but he sometimes Gages in Cistern, Couch, Floor and Kiln, and where he can make most, there he fixes his Charge: When the Malt is dryed, it must not cool on the Kiln, but be directly thrown off, not into a Heap, but spreaded wide in an airy place, till it is thoroughly cool, then put it into a Heap or otherwise dispose of it.

There are several methods used in drying of Malts, as the Iron Plate-frame, the Tyle-frame, that are both full of little Holes: The Brass-wyred and Iron-wyred Frame, and the Hair-cloth; the Iron and Tyled one, were chiefly Invented for drying of brown Malts and saving of Fuel, for these when they come to be thorough hot will make the Corns crack and jump by the fierceness of their heat, so that they will be roasted or scorch'd in a little time, and after they are off the Kiln, to plump the body of the Corn and make it take the Eye, some will sprinkle water over it that it may meet with the better Market. But if such Malt is not used quickly, it will slacken and lose its Spirits to a great degree, and perhaps in half a Year or less may be taken by the Whools and spoiled: Such hasty dryings or scorchings are also apt to bitter the Malt by burning its skin, and therefore these Kilns are not so much used now as formerly: The Wyre-frames indeed are

8

something better, yet they are apt to scorch the outward part of the Corn, that cannot be got off so soon as the Hair-cloth admits of, for these must be swept, when the other is only turned at once; however these last three ways are now in much request for drying pale and amber Malts, because their fire may be kept with more leisure, and the Malt more gradually and truer dyed, but by many the Hair-cloth is reckoned the best of all.

Malts are dryed with several sorts of Fuel; as the Coak, Welch-coal, Straw, Wood and Fern, &c. But the Coak is reckoned by most to exceed all others for making Drink of the finest Flavour and pale Colour, because it sends no smoak forth to hurt the Malt with any offensive tang, that Wood, Fern and Straw are apt to do in a lesser or greater degree; but there is a difference even in what is call'd Coak, the right sort being large Pit- coal chark'd or burnt in some measure to a Cinder, till all the Sulphur is consumed and evaporated away, which is called Coak, and this when it is truly made is the best of all other Fuels; but if there is but one Cinder as big as an Egg, that is not thoroughly cured, the smoak of this one is capable of doing a little damage, and this happens too often by the negligence or avarice of the Coak-maker: There is another sort by some wrongly called Coak, and rightly named Culme or Welch-coal, from *Swanzey* in *Pembrokeshire*, being of a hard stony substance in small bits resembling a shining Coal, and will burn without smoak, and by its sulphureous effluvia cast a most excellent whiteness on all the outward parts of the grainy body: In *Devonshire* I have seen their Marble or grey Fire-stone burnt into Lime with the strong fire that this Culme makes, and both this and the Chark'd Pit-coal affords a most sweet moderate and certain fire to all Malt that is dryed by it.

Straw is the next sweetest Fuel, but Wood and Fern worst of all.

Some I have known put a Peck or more of Peas, and malt them with five Quarters of Barley, and they'll greatly mellow the Drink, and so will Beans; but they won't come so soon, nor mix so conveniently with the Malt, as the Pea will.

I knew a Farmer, when he sends five Quarters of Barley to be Malted, puts in half a Peck or more of Oats amongst them, to prove he has justice done him by the Maker, who is hereby confin'd not to Change his Malt by reason others won't like such a mixture.

But there is an abuse sometimes committed by a necessitous Malster, who to come by Malt sooner than ordinary, makes use of Barley before it is thoroughly sweated in the Mow, and then it never makes right Malt, but will be steely and not yield a due quantity of wort, as I knew it once done by a Person that thrashed the Barley immediately from the Cart as it was brought out of the Field, but they that used its Malt suffered not a little, for it was impossible it should be good, because it did not thoroughly Chip or Spire on the floor, which caused this sort of Malt, when the water was put to it in the Mash-tub, to swell up and absorb the Liquor, but not return its due quantity again, as true Malt would, nor was the Drink of this Malt ever good in the Barrel, but remain'd a raw insipid beer, past the Art of Man to Cure, because this, like Cyder made from Apples directly off the Tree, that never sweated out their phlegmatick crude juice in the heap, cannot produce a natural Liquor from such unnatural management; for barley certainly is not fit to make Malt of until it is fully mellowed and sweated in the Mow, and the Season of the Year is ready for it, without both which there can be no assurance of good Malt: Several instances of this untimely making Malt I have known to happen, that has been the occasion of great quantities of bad Ales and Beers, for such Malt, retaining none of its Barley nature, or that the Season of the Year is not cold enough to admit of its natural working on the Floor, is not capable of producing a true Malt, it will cause its Drink to stink in the cask instead of growing fit for use, as not having its genuine Malt-nature to cure and preserve it, which all good Malts contribute to as well as the Hop.

There is another damage I have known accrue to the Buyer of Malt by Mellilet, a most stinking Weed that grows amongst some Barley, and is so mischievously predominant, as to taint it to a sad degree because its black Seed like that of an Onion, being lesser than the Barley, cannot be entirely separated, which obliges it to be malted with the Barley, and makes the Drink so heady that it is apt to fuddle the unwary by drinking a small quantity. This Weed is so natural to some Ground that the Farmer despairs of ever extirpating it, and is to be avoided as much as possible, because it very much hurts the Drink that is made from Malt mixed with it, by its nauseous Scent and Taste, as may be perceived by the Ointment made with it that bears its Name: I knew a Victualler that bought a parcel of Malt that this weed was amongst, and it spoiled all the Brewings and Sale of the Drink, for it's apt to cause Fevers, Colicks and other Distempers in the Body.

Darnel is a rampant Weed and grows much amongst some Barley, especially in the bad Husbandman's Ground, and most where it is sown with the Seed-barley: It does the least harm amongst Malt, because it adds a strength to it, and quickly intoxicates, if there is much in it; but where there is but little, the Malster regards it not, for the sake of its inebriating quality.

There are other Weeds or Seeds that annoy the Barley; but as the Screen, Sieve and throwing will take most of them out, there does not require here a Detail of their Particulars. Oats malted as Barley is, will make a weak, soft, mellow and pleasant Drink, but Wheat when done so, will produce a strong heady nourishing well-tasted and fine Liquor, which is now more practised then ever.

CHAP. III.

To know good from bad Malts.

This is a Matter of great Importance to all Brewers, both publick and private, for 'tis common for the Seller to cry all is good, but the Buyer's Case is different; wherefore it is prudential to endeavour to be Master of this Knowledge, but I have heard a great Malster that lived towards *Ware*, say, he knew a grand Brewer, that wetted near two hundred Quarters a Week, was not a judge of good and bad Malts, without which 'tis impossible to draw a true length of Ale or Beer.

To do this I know but of few Ways, *First*, By the Bite; Is to break the Malt Corn across between the Teeth, in the middle of it or at both Ends, and if it lasteth mellow and sweet, has a round body, breaks soft, is full of flower all its length, smells well and has a thin skin, then it is good; *Secondly*, By Water; Is to take a Glass near full, and put in some Malt; and if it swims, it is right, but if any sinks to the bottom, then it is not true Malt, but steely and retains somewhat of its Barley nature; yet I must own this is not an infallible Rule, because if a Corn of Malt is crack'd, split or broke, it will then take the water and sink, but there may an allowance be given for such incidents, and still room enough to make a judgment. *Thirdly*, Malt that is truly made will not be hard and steely, but of so mellow a Nature, that if forced against a dry Board, will mark and cast a white Colour almost like Chalk. *Fourthly*, Malt that is not rightly made will be part of it of a hard Barley nature, and weigh heavier than that which is true Malt.

CHAP. IV.

Of the Nature and Use of Pale, Amber and Brown Malts.

The pale Malt is the slowest and slackest dryed of any, and where it has had a leisure fire, a sufficient time allowed it on the Kiln, and a due care taken of it; the flower of the grain will remain in its full quantity, and thereby produce a greater length of wort, than the brown high dryed Malt, for which reason it is sold for one or two shillings *per* Quarter more than that: This pale Malt is also the most nutritious sort to the body of all others, as being in this state the most simple and nearest to its Original Barley-corn, that will retain an Alcalous and Balsamick quality much longer than the brown sort; the tender drying of this Malt bringing its body into so soft a texture of Parts, that most of the great Brewers, brew it with Spring and Well-waters, whose hard and binding Properties they think agrees best with this loose-bodied Malt, either in Ales or Beer's and which will also dispense with hotter waters in brewing of it, than the brown Malt can. The amber-colour'd Malt is that which is dryed in a medium degree, between the pale and the brown, and is very much in use, as being free of either extream. Its colour is pleasant, its taste agreeable and its nature wholsome, which makes it be prefer'd by many as the best of Malts; this by some is brewed either with hard or soft waters, or a mixture of both.

The brown Malt is the soonest and highest dryed of any, even till it is so hard, that it's difficult to bite some of its Corns asunder, and is often so crusted or burnt, that the farinous part loses a great deal of its essential Salts and vital Property, which frequently deceives its ignorant Brewer, that hopes to draw as much Drink from a quarter of this, as he does from pale or amber sorts: This Malt by some is thought to occasion the Gravel and Stone, besides what is commonly called the Heart-burn; and is by its steely nature less nourishing than the pale or amber Malts, being very much impregnated with the fiery fumiferous Particles of the Kiln, and therefore its Drink sooner becomes sharp and acid than that made from the pale or amber sorts, if they are all fairly brewed: For this reason the *London* Brewers mostly use the *Thames* or *New River* waters to brew

11

this Malt with, for the sake of its soft nature, whereby it agrees with the harsh qualities of it better than any of the well or other hard Sorts, and makes a luscious Ale for a little while, and a But-beer that will keep very well five or six Months, but after that time it generally grows stale, notwithstanding there be ten or twelve Bushels allowed to the Hogshead, and it be hopp'd accordingly.

Pale and amber Malts dryed with Coak or Culm, obtains a more clean bright pale Colour than if dryed with any other Fuel, because there is not smoak to darken and sully their Skins or Husks, and give them an ill relish, that those Malts little or more have, which are dryed with Straw, Wood, or Fern, &c. The Coak or *Welch* Coal also makes more true and compleat Malt, as I have before hinted, than any other Fuel, because its fire gives both a gentle and certain Heat, whereby the Corns are in all their Parts gradually dryed, and therefore of late these Malts have gained such a Reputation that great quantities have been consumed in most Parts of the Nation for their wholsome Natures and sweet fine Taste: These make such fine Ales and But-beers, as has tempted several of our Malsters in my Neighbour-hood to burn Coak or Culm at a great expence of Carriage thirty Miles from *London*.

Next to the Coak-dryed Malt, the Straw-dryed is the sweetest and best tasted: This I must own is sometimes well Malted where the Barley, Wheat, Straw, Conveniencies and the Maker's Skill are good; but as the fire of the Straw is not so regular as the Coak, the Malt is attended with more uncertainty in its making, because it is difficult to keep it to a moderate and equal Heat, and also exposes the Malt in some degree to the taste of the smoak.

Brown Malts are dryed with Straw, Wood and Fern, &c. the Straw-dryed is not the best, but the Wood sort has a most unnatural Taste, that few can bear with, but the necessitous, and those that are accustomed to its strong smoaky tang; yet is it much used in some of the Western Parts of *England*, and many thousand Quarters of this Malt has been formerly used in *London* for brewing the Butt-keeping-beers with, and that because it sold for two Shillings *per* Quarter cheaper than the Straw-dryed Malt, nor was this Quality of the Wood-dryed Malt much regarded by some of its Brewers, for that its ill Taste is lost in nine or twelve Months, by the Age of the Beer, and the strength of the great Quantity of Hops that were used in its Preservation.

The Fern-dryed Malt is also attended with a rank disagreeable Taste from the smoak of this Vegetable, with which many Quarters of Malt are dryed, as appears by the great Quantities annually cut by Malsters on our Commons, for the two prevalent Reasons of cheapness and plenty.

At *Bridport* in *Dorsetshire*, I knew an Inn-keeper use half Pale and half Brown Malt for Brewing his Butt-beers, that, proved to my Palate the best I ever drank on the Road, which I think may be accounted for, in that the Pale being the slackest, and the Brown the hardest dryed, must produce a mellow good Drink by the help of a requisite Age, that will reduce those extreams to a proper Quality.

CHAP. V.

Of the Nature of several Waters and their use in Brewing. And first of Well-waters.

Water next to Malt is what by course comes here under Consideration as a Matter of great Importance in Brewing of wholsome fine Malt-liquors, and is of such Consequence that it concerns every one to know the nature of the water he Brews with, because it is the Vehicle by which the nutritious and pleasant Particles of the Malt and Hop are conveyed into our Bodies, and there becomes a diluter of our Food: Now the more simple and freer every water is from foreign Particles, the better it will answer those Ends and Purposes; for, as Dr_.Mead_ observes, some waters are so loaded with stony Corpuscles, that even the Pipes thro' which they are carried, in time are incrusted and stopt up by them, and is of that petrifying nature as to breed the Stone in the Bladder, which many of the *Parisians* have been instances of, by using this sort of water out of the River *Seine.* And of this Nature is another at *Rowel* in *Northamptonshire*, which in no great distance of time so clogs the Wheel of an overshot Mill there, that they are forced with, convenient Instruments to cut way for its Motion; and what makes it still more evident, is the sight of those incrusted Sides of the Tea-kettles, that the hard Well-waters are the occasion of, by being often boiled in them: And it is further related by the same Doctor, that a Gentlewoman afflicted with frequent returns of violent Colick Pains was cured by the Advice of *Van Helmont*, only by leaving off drinking Beer brewed with Well-water; It's true, such a fluid has a greater force and aptness to extract the tincture out of Malt, than is to be had in the more innocent and soft Liquor of Rivers: But for this very reason it ought not, unless upon meer necessity, to be made use of; this Quality being owing to the mineral Particles and alluminous Salts with which it is impregnated. For these waters thus saturated, will by their various gravities in circulation, deposit themselves in one part of the animal Body or other, which has made some prove the goodness of Water by the lightness of its body in the Water Scales, now sold in several of the *London* Shops, in order to avoid the Scorbutick, Colicky, Hypochondriack, and other ill Effects of the Clayey and other gross Particles of stagnating Well-waters, and the calculous Concretions of others; and therefore such waters ought to be mistrusted more than any, where they are not pure clear and soft or that don't arise from good Chalks or stony Rocks, that are generally allowed to afford the best of all the Well sorts.

Spring-waters are in general liable to partake of those minerals thro' which they pass, and are salubrious or mischievous accordingly. At *Uppingham* in *Rutland*, their water is said to come off an Allum-rock, and so tints their Beer with its saline Quality, that it is easily tasted at the first Draught. And at *Dean* in *Northamptonshire*, I have seen the very Stones colour the rusty Iron by the constant running of a Spring-water; but that which will Lather with Soap, or such soft water that percolates through Chalk, or a Grey Fire-stone, is generally accounted best, for Chalks in this respect excell all other Earths, in that it administers nothing unwholsome to the perfluent waters, but undoubtedly absorps by its drying spungy Quality any ill minerals that may accompany the water that runs thro' them. For which reason they throw in, great Quantities of Chalk into their Wells at *Ailsbury* to soften their water, which coming off a black Sand-stone, is so hard and sharp that it will often turn their Beer sour in a Week's time, so that in its Original State it's neither fit to Wash nor Brew with, but so long as the Alcalous soft Particles of the Chalk holds good, they put it to both uses.

River-waters are less liable to be loaded with metallick, petrifying, saline and other insanous Particles of the Earth, than the Well or Spring sorts are, especially at some distance from the Spring-head, because the Rain water mixes with and softens it, and are also much cured by the Sun's heat and the Air's power, for which reason I have known several so strict, that they won't let their Horses drink near the first rise of some of them; this I have seen the sad Effects of, and which has obliged me to avoid two that run cross a Road in *Bucks* and *Hertfordshire*: But in their runnings they often collect gross Particles from ouzy muddy mixtures, particularly near Town, that make the Beer subject to new fermentations, and grow foul upon alteration of weather as the *Thames* water generrly does; yet is this for its softness much better than the hard sort, however both these waters are used by some Brewers as I shall hereafter observe; but where a River-water can be had clear in a dry time, when no great Rain has lately fell out of Rivulets or Rivers that have a Gravelly, Chalky, Sandy or Stone-bottom free from the Disturbance of Cattle, &c. and in good Air, as that of *Barkhamstead St. Peters* in *Hertfordshire* is; it may then justly claim the name of a most excellent water for Brewing, and will make a stronger Drink with the same quantity of Malt than any of the Well-waters; insomuch that that of the *Thames* has been proved to make as strong Beer with seven Bushels of Malt, as Well-water with eight; and so are all River-waters in a proportionable degree, and where they can be obtain'd clean and pure, Drink may be drawn fine in a few Days after Tunning.

Rain-water is very soft, of a most simple and pure nature, and the best Diluter of any, especially if received free from Dirt, and the Salt of Mortar that often mixes with it as it runs off tyled Roofs; this is very agreeable for brewing of Ales that are not to be kept a great while, but for Beers that are to remain some time in the Casks, it is not so, well, as being apt to putrify the soonest of any.

Pond-waters; this includes all standing waters chiefly from Rain, and are good or bad as they happen; for where there is a clean bottom, and the water lies undisturbed from the tread of Cattle, or too many Fish, in an open sound Air, in a large quantity, and where the Sun has free access; it then comes near, if not quite as good as Rain or River-waters, as is that of *Blew-pot* Pond on the high Green at *Gaddesden* in *Hertfordshire* and many others, which are often prefer'd for Brewing, even beyond many of the soft Well-waters about them. But where it is in a small quantity, or full of Fish (especially the sling Tench) or is so disturbed by Cattle as to force up Mud and Filth; it is then the most foul and disagreeable of all others: So is it likewise in long dry Seasons when our Pond-waters are so low as obliges us to strain it thro' Sieves before we can use it, to take out the small red Worms and other Corruptions, that our stagnant waters are generally then too full of. The latest and best Doctors have so far scrutinized into the primo Cause of our *British* malady the Scurvy, as to affirm its first rise is from our unwholesome stagnating waters, and especially those that come off a clayey surface, as there are about *Londonderry* and *Amsterdam*, for that where the waters are worst, there this Distemper is most common, so that in their Writings they have put it out of all doubt, that most of our complicated symptoms that are rank'd under this general Name, if they don't take their beginning from such water, do own it to be their chief Cause.

CHAP. VI.

Of Grinding Malts.

As trifling as this Article in Brewing may seem at first it very worthily deserves the notice of all concern'd therein, for on this depends much the good of our Drink, because if it is ground too small the flower of the Malt will be the easier and more freely mix with the water, and then will cause the wort to run thick, and therefore the Malt must be only just broke in the Mill, to make it emit its Spirit gradually, and incorporate its flower with the water in such a manner that first a stout Beer, then an Ale, and afterwards a small Beer may be had at one and the same Brewing, and the wort run off fine and clear to the last. Many are likewise so sagacious as to grind their brown Malt a Fortnight before they use it, and keep it in a dry Place from the influence of too moist an Air, that it may become mellower by losing in a great measure the fury of its harsh fiery Particles, and its steely nature, which this sort of Malt acquires on the Kiln; however this as well as many other hard Bodies may be reduced by Time and Air into a more soluble, mellow and soft Condition, and then it will imbibe the water and give a natural kind tincture more freely, by which a greater quantity and stronger Drink may be made, than if it was used directly from the Mill, and be much smoother and better tasted. But the pale Malt will be fit for use at a Week's end, because the leisureness of their drying endows them with a softness from the time they are taken off the Kiln to the time they are brewed, and supplies in them what Time and Air must do in the brown sorts. This method of grinding Malt so long before-hand can't be so conveniently practised by some of the great Brewers, because several of them Brew two or three times a Week, but now most of them out of good Husbandry grind their Malts into the Tun by the help of a long descending wooden Spout, and here they save the Charge of emptying or uncasing it out of the Bin (which formerly they used to do before this new way was discovered) and also the waste of a great deal of the Malt-flower that was lost when carryed in Baskets, whereas now the Cover of the Tun presents all that Damage In my common Brewhouse at *London* I ground my Malt between two large Stones by the Horse-mill that with one Horse would grind [blank space] quarters an Hour, But in the Country I use a steel Hand-mill, that Cost at first forty Shillings; which will by the help of only one Man grind six or eight Bushels in an Hour, and will last a Family many Years without hardning or cutting: There are some old-fashion'd stone Hand-mills in being, that some are Votaries for and prefer to the Iron ones, because they alledge that these break the Corn's body, when the Iron ones only cut it in two, which occasions the Malt so broke by the Stones, to give the water a more easy, free and regular Power to extract its Virtue, than the Cut-malt can that is more confin'd within its Hull. Notwithstanding the Iron ones are now mostly in Use for their great Dispatch and long Duration. In the Country it is frequently done by some to throw a Sack of Malt on a Stone or Brick-floor as soon as it is ground, and there let it lye, giving it one turn, for a Day or two, that the Stones or Bricks may draw out the fiery Quality it received from the Kiln, and give the Drink a soft mild Taste.

CHAP. VII.

Of Brewing in general.

Brewing, like several other Arts is prostituted to the opinionated Ignorance of many conceited Pretenders, who if they have but seen or been concern'd in but one Brewing, and that only one Bushel of Malt, assume the Name of a Brewer and dare venture on several afterwards, as believing it no other Task, than more Labour, to Brew a great deal as well as a little; from hence it partly is, that we meet with such hodge-podge Ales and Beers, as are not only disagreeable in Taste and Foulness, but indeed unwholsome to the Body of Man, for as it is often drank thick and voided thin, the Feces or gross part must in my Opinion remain behind in some degree. Now what the Effects of that may be, I must own I am not Physician enough to explain, but shrewdly suspect it may be the Cause of Stones, Colicks, Obstructions, and several other Chronical Distempers; for if we consider that the sediments of Malt-liquors are the refuse of a corrupted Grain, loaded with the igneous acid Particles of the Malt, and then again with the corrosive sharp Particles of the Yeast, it must consequently be very pernicious to the *British* human Body especially, which certainly suffers much from the animal Salts of the great Quantities of Flesh that we Eat more than People of any other Nation whatsoever; and therefore are more then ordinarily obligated not to add the scorbutick mucilaginous Qualities of such gross unwholsome Particles, that every one makes a lodgment of in their Bodies, as the Liquors they drink are more or less thick; for in plain Truth, no Malt-liquor can be good without it's fine. The late Curious *Simon Harcourt* Esq; of *Penly,* whom I have had the honour to drink some of his famous *October* with, thought the true Art of Brewing of such Importance, that it is said to Cost him near twenty Pounds to have an old Days-man taught it by a *Welch* Brewer, and sure it was this very Man exceeded all others in these Parts afterwards in the Brewing of that which he called his October_ Beer. So likewise in *London* they lay such stress on this Art, that many have thought it worth their while to give one or two hundred Guineas with an Apprentice: This Consideration also made an Ambassador give an extraordinary Encouragement to one of my Acquaintance to go over with him, that was a great Master of this Science. But notwithstanding all that can be said that relates to this Subject, there are so many Incidents attending Malt-liquors, that it has puzled several expert Men to account for their difference, though brewed by the same Brewer, with the same Malt, Hops and Water, and in the same Month and Town, and tapp'd at the same time: The Beer of one being fine, strong and well Tasted, while the others have not had any worth drinking, now this may be owing to the different Weather in the same Month, that might cause an Alteration in the working of the Liquors, or that the Cellar may not be so convenient, or that the Water was more disturbed by Winds or Rains, &c. But it has been observed that where a Gentleman has imployed one Brewer constantly, and uses the same sort of Ingredients, and the Beer kept in dry Vaults or Cellars that have two or three Doors; the Drink has been generally good. And where such Malt-liquors are kept in Butts, more time is required to ripen, meliorate and fine them, than those kept in Hogsheads, because the greater quantity must have the longer time; so also a greater quantity will preserve itself better than a lesser one, and on this account the Butt and Hogshead are the two best sized Casks of all others; but all under a Hogshead hold rather too small a quantity to keep their Bodies. The Butt is certainly a most noble Cask for this use, as being generally set upright, whereby it maintains a large Cover of Yeast, that greatly contributes to the keeping in the Spirits of the Beer, admits of a most convenient broaching in the middle and its lower part, and by its broad level Bottom, gives a better lodgment to the fining and preserving Ingredients, than any other Cask whatsoever that lyes in, the long Cross-form. Hence it partly is, that the common Butt-beer is at this time in greater Reputation than ever in *London*, and the Home-brew'd Drinks out of Credit; because the first is better cured in its Brewing, in its Quantity, in its Cask, and in its Age; when the latter has been loaded with the pernicious Particles of great Quantities of Yeast, of a short Age, and kept in small Casks, that confines its Owner, only to Winter Brewing and Sale, as not being capable of sustaining the Heat of the Weather, for that the acidity of the Yeast brings on a sudden hardness and staleness of the Ale, which to preserve in its mild Aley Taste, will not admit of any great Quantity of Hops; and this is partly the reason that the handful of Salt which the *Plymouth* Brewers put into their Hogshead, hinders their Ale from keeping, as I shall hereafter take notice of.

CHAP. VIII.

The London *Method of Brewing.*

In a great Brewhouse that I was concern'd in, they wetted or used a considerable Quantity of Malt in one Week in Brewing Stout-beer, common Butt-beer, Ale and small Beer, for which purpose they have River and Well Waters, which they take in several degrees of Heat, as the Malt, Goods and Grain are in a condition to receive them, and according to the Practice there I shall relate the following Particulars, viz.

For Stout Butt Beer.

This is the strongest Butt-Beer that is Brewed from brown Malt, and often sold for forty Shillings the Barrel, or six Pound the Butt out of the wholesale Cellars:

17

The Liquor (for it is Sixpence forfeit in the *London* Brewhouse if the word Water is named) in the Copper designed for the first Mash, has a two Bushel Basket, or more, of the most hully Malt throw'd over it, to cover its Top and forward its Boiling; this must be made very hot, almost ready to boil, yet not so as to blister, for then it will be in too high a Heat; but as an indication of this, the foul part of the Liquor will ascend, and the Malt swell up, and then it must be parted, look'd into and felt with the Finger or back of the Hand, and if the Liquor is clear and can but be just endured, it is then enough, and the Stoker must damp his fire as soon as possible by throwing in a good Parcel of fresh Coals, and shutting his Iron vent Doors, if there are any; immediately on this they let as much cold Liquor or Water run into the Copper as will make it all of a Heat, somewhat more than Blood-warm, this they Pump over, or let it pass by a Cock into an upright wooden square Spout or Trunk, and it directly rises thro' the Holes of a false Bottom into the Malt, which is work'd by several Men with Oars for about half an Hour, and is called the first and stiff Mash: While this is doing, there is more Liquor heating in the Copper that must not be let into the mash Tun till it is very sharp, almost ready to boil, with this they Mash again, then cover it with several Baskets of Malt, and let it stand an Hour before it runs into the Under-back, which when boiled an Hour and a half with a good quantity of Hops makes this Stout. The next is Mash'd with a cooler Liquor, then a sharper, and the next Blood-warm or quite Cold; by which alternate degrees of Heat, a Quantity of small Beer is made after the Stout.

For Brewing strong brown Ale called Stitch.

This is most of it the first running of the Malt, but yet of a longer Length than is drawn for the Stout; It has but few Hops boiled in it, and is sold for Eight-pence *per* Gallon at the Brewhouse out of the Tun, and is generally made to amend the common brown Ale with, on particular Occasions. This Ale I remember was made use of by [Blank space] *Medlicot* Esq; in the beginning of a Consumption, and I heard him say, it did him very great Service, for he lived many Years afterwards.

For Brewing common brown Ale and Starting Beer.

They take the Liquors from the brown Ale as for the Stout, but draw a greater Quantity from the Malt, than for Stout or Stitch, and after the fifth and second Mash they Cap the Goods with fresh Malt to keep in the Spirit and Boil it an Hour; after this, small Beer is made of the same Goods. Thus also the common brown Starting Butt-Beer is Brewed, only boiled with more Hops an Hour and a half, and work'd cooler and longer than the brown Ale, and a shorter Length drawn from the Malt. But it is often practised after the brown Ale, and where a Quantity of small Beer is wanted, or that it is to be Brewed better than ordinary, to put so much fresh Malt on the Goods as will answer that purpose.

For Brewing Pale and Amber Ales and Beers.

As the brown Malts are Brewed with River, these are Brewed with Well or Spring Liquors. The Liquors are by some taken sharper for pale than brown Malts, and after the first scalding Liquor is put over, some lower the rest by degrees to the last which is quite Cold, for their small Beer; so also for Butt-Beers there is no other difference than the addition of more Hops, and bulling, and the method of working. But the reasons for Brewing pale Malts with Spring or hard Well waters, I have mentioned in my second Book of Brewing.

For Brewing Entire Guile Small Beer.

On the first Liquor they throw some hully Malt to shew the break of it, and when it is very sharp, they let in some cold Liquor, and run it into the Tun milk warm; this is mash'd with thirty or forty pulls of the Oar, and let stand till the second Liquor is ready, which must be almost scalding hot to the back of the Hand, then run it by the Cock into the Tun, mash it up and let it stand an Hour before it is spended off into the Under-back: These two pieces of Liquor will make one Copper of the first wort, without putting any fresh Malt on the Goods; the next Liquor to be Blood-warm, the next sharp, and the next cool or cold; for the general way in great Brewhouses is to let a cool Liquor precede a sharp one, because it gradually opens the Pores of the Malt and Goods, and prepares the way for the hotter Liquor that is to follow.

The several Lengths or Quantities of Drinks that have been made from Malt, and their several Prices, as they have been sold at a common Brewhouse.

For Stout-Beer, is commonly drawn one Barrel off a quarter of Malt, and sold for thirty Shillings *per* Barrel from the Tun. For Stitch or strong brown Ale, one Barrel and a Firkin, at one and twenty Shillings and Fourpence *per* Barrel from the Tun. For common brown Ale, one Barrel and a half or more, at sixteen Shillings *per* Barrel, that holds thirty two Gallons, from the Tun. For Intire small Beer, five or six Barrels off a Quarter, at seven or eight Shillings *per* Barrel from the Tun. For Pale and Amber Ale, one Barrel and a Firkin, at one Shilling *per* Gallon from the Tun.

CHAP. IX.

The Country or private way of Brewing.

Several Countries have their several Methods of Brewing, as is practised in *Wales, Dorchester, Nottingham, Dundle*, and many other Places; but evading Particulars, I shall here recommend that which I think is most serviceable both in Country and *London* private Families. And first, I shall observe that the great Brewer has some advantages in Brewing more than the small one, and yet the latter has some Conveniences which the former can't enjoy; for 'tis certain that the great Brewer can make more Drink, and draw a greater Length in proportion to his Malt, than a Person can from a lesser Quantity, because the greater the Body, the more is its united Power in receiving and discharging, and he can Brew with less charge and trouble by means of his more convenient Utensils. But then the private Brewer is not without his Benefits; for he can have his Malt ground at pleasure, his Tubs and moveable Coolers sweeter and better clean'd than the great fixed Tuns and Backs, he can skim off his top Yeast and leave his bottom Lees behind, which is what the great Brewer can't so well do; he can at discretion make additions of cold wort to his too forward Ales and Beers, which the great Brewer can't so conveniently do; he can Brew how and when he pleases, which the great ones are in some measure hindred from. But to come nearer the matter, I will suppose a private Family to Brew five Bushels of Malt, whose Copper holds brim-full thirty six Gallons or a Barrel: On this water we put half a Peck of Bran or Malt when it is something hot, which will much forward it by keep in the Steams or Spirit of the water, and when it begins to Boil, if the water is foul, skim off the Bran or Malt and give it the Hogs, or else lade both water and that into the mash Vat, where it is to remain till the steam is near spent, and you can see your Face in it, which will be in about a quarter of an Hour in cold weather; then let all but half a Bushel of the Malt run very leisurely into it, stirring it all the while with an Oar or Paddle, that it may not Ball, and when the Malt is all but just mix'd with water it is enough, which I am sensible is different from the old way and the general present Practice; but I shall here clear that Point. For by not stirring or mashing the Malt into a Pudding Consistence or thin Mash, the Body of it lies in a more loose Condition, that will easier and sooner admit of a quicker and more true Passage of the after- ladings of the several Bowls or Jets of hot water, which must run thorough it before the Brewing is ended; by which free percolation the water has ready access to all the parts of the broken Malt, so that the Brewer is capacitated to Brew quicker or slower, and to make more Ale or small Beer; If more Ale, then hot Boiling water must be laded over to slow that one Bowl must run almost off before another is put over, which will occasion the whole Brewing to last about sixteen Hours, especially if the *Dundle* way is followed, of spending it out of the Tap as small as a Straw, and as fine as Sack, and then it will be quickly so in the Barrel: Of if less or weaker Ale is to be made and good small Beer, then the second Copper of boiling water may be put over expeditiously and drawn out with a large and fast steam. After the first stirring of the Malt is done, then put over the reserve of half a Bushel of fresh Malt to the four Bushels and half that is already in the Tub, which must be spread all over it, and also cover the top of the Tub with some Sacks or other Cloths to keep in the Steam or Spirit of the Malt; then let it stand two or three Hours, at the end of which, put over now and then a Bowl of the boiling water in the Copper as is before directed, and so continue to do till as much is run off as will almost fill the Copper; then in a Canvas or other loose woven Cloth, put in half a Pound of Hops and boil them half an Hour, when they must be taken out, and as many fresh ones put in their room as is judged proper to boil half an Hour more, if for Ale: But if for keeping Beer, half a Pound of fresh ones should be put in at every half Hour's end, and Boil an Hour and a half briskly: Now while the first Copper of wort is Boiling, there should be scalding water leisurely put over the Goods, Bowl by Bowl, and run off, that the Copper may be filled again immediately after the first is out, and boiled an Hour with near the same quantity of fresh Hops, and in the same manner as those in the first Copper of Ale- wort were. The rest for small Beer may be all cold water put over the Grains at once, or at twice, and Boil'd an Hour each Copper with the Hops that has been boil'd before. But here I must observe, that sometimes I have not an opportunity to get hot water for making all my second Copper of wort, which obliges me then to make use of cold to supply what was wanting. Out of five Bushels of Malt, I generally make a Hogshead of Ale with the two first Coppers of wort, and a Hogshead of small Beer with the other two, but this more or less according to please me, always taking Care to let each Copper of wort be strained off thro' a Sieve, and cool in four or five Tubs to prevent its foxing. Thus I have brewed many Hogsheads of midling Ale that when the Malt is good, has proved strong enough for myself and satisfactory to my friends: But for strong keeping Beer, the first Copper of wort may be wholly put to that use, and all the rest small Beer: Or when the first Copper of wort is intirely made use of for strong Beer, the Goods may be help'd with more fresh Malt (according to the *London* Fashion) and water lukewarm put over at first with the Bowl, but soon after sharp or boiling water, which may make a Copper of good Ale, and small Beer after that. In some Parts of the North, they take one or more Cinders red hot and throw some Salt on them to overcome the Sulphur of the Coal, and then directly thrust it into the fresh Malt or Goods, where it lies till all the water is laded over and the Brewing done, for there is only one or two mashings or stirrings at most necessary in a Brewing: Others that Brew with Wood will quench one or more Brands ends of Ash in a Copper of wort, to mellow the Drink as a burnt Toast of Bread does a Pot of Beer; but it is to be observed, that this must not be done with Oak, Firr, or any other strong-scented Wood; lest it does more harm than good.

Another Way.

When small Beer is not wanted, and another Brewing is soon to succeed the former, then may the last small Beer wort, that has had no Hops boiled in it, remain in the Copper all Night, which will prevent its foxing, and be ready to boil instead of so much water to put over the next fresh Malt: This will greatly contribute to the strengthening, bettering and colouring of the next wort, and is commonly used in this manner when Stout or *October* Beer is to be made, not that it is less serviceable if it was for Ale, or Intire Guile small Beer; but lest it should taste of the Copper by remaining all Night in it, it may be dispersed into Tubs and kept a Week or more together if some fresh cold water is daily added to it, and may be brewed as I have mentioned, taking particular Care in this as well as in the former ways to return two, three, or more Hand-bowls of wort into the Mash Tub, that first of all runs off, till it comes absolutely fine and clear, and then it may spend away or run off for good: Others will reserve this small Beer wort unboiled in Tubs, and keep it there a Week in Winter, or two or three Days in Summer, according to Conveniency, by putting fresh water every Day to it, and use it instead of water for the first Mash, alledging it is better so than boiled, because by that it is thickened and will cause the wort to run foul; this may be a Benefit to a Victualler that Brews to Sell again, and can't Vent his small Beer; because for such small raw wort that is mix'd with any water, there is no Excise to be pay'd.

For Brewing Intire Guile Small Beer.

There can be no way better for making good small Beer, than by Brewing it from fresh Malt, because in Malt as well as in Hops, and so in all other Vegetables, there is a Spirituous and Earthy part, as I shall further enlarge on in writing of the Hop; therefore all Drink brewed from Goods or Grains after the first or second worts are run off, is not so good and wholsome, as that intirely brewed from fresh Malt, nor could any thing but Necessity cause me to make use of such Liquor; yet how many thousands are there in this Nation that know nothing of the matter, tho' it is of no small Importance, and ought to be regarded by all those that value their Health and Taste. And here I advertise every one who reads or hears this, and is capable of being his own Friend, so far to mind this *Item* and prefer that small Beer which is made entirely from fresh Malt, before any other that is brewed after strong Beer or Ale. Now to brew such Guile small Beer after the boiling water has stood in the Tub till it is clear, put in the Malt leisurely, and mash it that it does not Ball or Clot, then throw over some fresh Malt on the Top, and Cloths over that, and let it stand two Hours before it is drawn off, the next water may be between hot and cold, the next boiling hot, and the next Cold; or if conveniency allows not, there may be once scalding water, and all the rest cold instead of the last three. Thus I brew my Intire Guile small Beer, by putting the first and last worts together, allowing half, or a Pound of Hops to a Hogshead and boiling it one Hour, but if the Hops were shifted twice in that time, the Drink would plainly discover the benefit. Sometimes, when I have been in haste for small Beer, I have put half a Bushel of Malt and a few Hops into my Barrel-Copper, and boil'd a Kettle gallop as some call it an Hour, and made me a present Drink, till I had more leisure to brew better.

A particular way of Brewing strong October *Beer.*

There was a Man in this Country that brewed for a Gentleman constantly after a Very precise Method, and that was, as soon as he had put over all his first Copper of water and mash'd it some time, he would directly let the Cock run a small stream and presently put some fresh Malt on the former, and mash on the while the Cock was spending, which he would put again over the Malt, as often as his Pail or Hand-bowl was full, and this for an Hour or two together; then he would let it run off intirely, and put it over at once, to run off again as small as a Straw. This was for his *October* Beer: Then he would put scalding water over the Goods at once, but not mash, and Cap them with more fresh Malt that stood an Hour undisturbed before he would draw it off for Ale; the rest was hot water put over the Goods and mash'd at twice for small Beer: And it was observed that his *October* Beer was the most famous in the Country, but his Grains good for little, for that he had by this method wash'd out all or most of their goodness; this Man was a long while in Brewing, and once his Beer did not work in the Barrel for a Month in a very hard Frost, yet when the weather broke it recovered and fermented well, and afterwards proved very good Drink, but he seldom work'd, his Beer less than a Week in the Vat, and was never tapp'd under three Years.

This way indeed is attended with extraordinary Labour and Time, by the Brewers running off the wort almost continually, and often returning the same again into the mash Vat, but then it certainly gives him an opportunity of extracting and washing out the goodness of the Malt, more than any of the common Methods, by which he is capacitated to make his *October* or *March* Beer as strong as he pleases. The Fame of *Penly October* Beer is at this time well known not only throughout *Hertfordshire*, but several other remote Places, and truly not without desert, for in all my Travels I never met with any that excell'd it, for a clear amber Colour, a fine relish, and a light warm digestion. But what excell'd all was the generosity of its Donor, who for Hospitality in his Viands and this *October* Beer, has left but few of his Fellows. I remember his usual Expression to be, You are welcome to a good Batch of my *October*, and true it was, that he proved his Words by his Deeds, for not only the rich but even the poor Man's Heart was generally made glad, even in advance, whenever they had Business at *Penly*, as expecting a refreshment of this Cordial Malt Liquor, that often was accompany'd with a good Breakfast or Dinner besides, while several others that had greater Estates would seem generous by giving a Yeoman Man Neighbour, the Mathematical Treat of a look on the Spit, and a standing Drink at the Tap.

Of Brewing Molosses Beer.

Molosses or Treacle has certainly been formerly made too much use of in the brewing of Stout Beer, common Butt Beers, brown Ales and small Beer when Malts have been dear: But it is now prohibited under the Penalty of fifty Pounds for every ten Pounds weight found in any common Brewhouse, and as Malts are now about twenty Shillings *per* Quarter, and like to be so by the Blessing of God, and the Assistance of that invaluable excellent Liquor for steeping Seed Barley in, published in a late Book intituled, *Chiltern and Vale Farming Explained*: There is no great danger of that, Imposition being rife again, which in my Opinion was very unwholsome, because the Brewer was obliged to put such a large quantity of Treacle into his water or small wort to make it strong Beer or Ale, as very probably raised a sweating in some degree in the Body of the drinker: Tho' in small Beer a lesser quantity will serve; and therefore I have known some to brew it in that for their Health's sake, because this does not breed the Scurvy like Malt-liquors, and at the same time will keep open the Pipes and Passages of the Lungs and Stomach, for which purpose they put in nine Pounds weight into a Barrel-Copper of cold water, first mixing it well, and boiling it briskly with a quarter of a Pound of Hops or more one Hour, so that it may come off twenty seven Gallons.

A Method practiced by a Victualler for Brewing of Ale or October *Beer from* Nottingham.

His Copper holds twenty four Gallons, and the Mash Tub has room enough for four and more Bushels of Malt. The first full Copper of boiling water he puts into the Mash Tub, there to lye a quarter of an Hour, till the steam is so far spent, that he can see his Face in it, or as soon as the hot water is put in, throws a Pail or two of cold water into it, which will bring it at once into a temper; then he lets three Bushels of Malt be run leisurely into it, and stirred or mash'd all the while, but as little as can be, or no more than just to keep the Malt from clotting or balling; when that is done, he puts one Bushel of dry Malt on the Top to keep in the Vapour or Spirit, and so lets it stand covered two Hours, or till the next

23

Copper full of water is boiled hot, which he lades over the Malt or Goods three Hand-bowls full at a time, that are to run off at the Cock or Tap by a very small stream before more is put on, which again must be returned into the Mash Tub till it comes off exceeding fine, for unless the wort is clear when it goes into the Copper, there are little hopes it will be so in the Barrel, which leisure way obliges him to be sixteen Hours in brewing these four Bushels of Malt. Now between the ladings over he puts cold water into the Copper to be boiling hot, while the other is running off; by this means his Copper is kept up near full, and the Cock spending to the end of brewing his Ale or small Beer, of which only twenty one Gallons must be saved of the first wort that is reserved in a Tub, wherein four Ounces of Hops are put and then it is to be set by. For the second wort I will suppose there are twenty Gallons of water in the Copper boiling hot, that must be all laded over in the same manner as the former was, but no cold water need here be mixed; when half of this is run out into a Tub, it must be directly put into the Copper with half of the first wort, strain'd thro' the Brewing Sieve as it lies on a small loose wooden Frame over the Copper, to keep back those Hops that were first put in to preserve it, which is to make the first Copper twenty one Gallons; then upon its beginning to boil he puts in a Pound of Hops in one or two Canvas or other coarse Linnen Bags, somewhat larger than will just contain the Hops, that an allowance may be given for their swell; this he boils away very briskly for half an Hour, when he takes the Hops out and continues boiling the wort by itself till it breaks into Particles a little ragged, and then it is enough and must be dispers'd into the cooling Tubs very thin: Then put the remainder of the first and second wort together and boil that, the same time, in the same manner, and with the same quantity of fresh Hops the first was. The rest of the third or small Beer wort will be about fifteen or twenty Gallons more or less, he mixes directly with some cold water to keep it free of Excise, and puts it into the Copper as the first Liquor to begin a second Brewing of Ale with another four Bushels of Malt as he did before, and so on for several Days together if necessary; but at last there may be some small Beer made, tho' some will make make none, because the Goods or Grains will go the further in feeding of Hogs.

Observations on the foregoing Method.

The first Copper of twenty four Gallons of water is but sufficient to wet three Bushels of Malt, and by the additions of cold water as the hot is expended, it matters not how much the Malt drinks up: Tho' a third part of water is generally allowed for that purpose that is never returned.

By the leisure putting over the Bowls of water, the goodness of the Malt is the more extracted and washed out, so that more Ale may be this way made and less small Beer, than if the wort was drawed out hastily; besides the wort has a greater opportunity of coming off finer by a slow stream than by a quicker one, which makes this Method excel all others that discharge the wort out of the Mash Tub more hastily. Also by the continual running of the Cock or Tap, the Goods or Grains are out of danger of sowring, which often happens in Summer Brewings, especially when the Cook is stopt between the several boilings of the wort, and what has been the very Cause of damaging or spoiling many Guiles of

Drink.

This Brewer reposes such a Confidence in the Hops to preserve the wort from fixing even in the very hottest time in Summer, that he puts all his first running into one Tub, till he has an opportunity of boiling it, and when Tubs and Room are so scarce that the wort is obliged to be laid thick to cool, then the security of some fresh Hops (and not them already boiled or soak'd) may be put into it, which may be got out again by letting the Drink run thro' the Cullender, and after that a Hair Sieve to keep the Seeds of the Hop back as the Drink goes into the Barrel: But this way of putting Hops into the cooling Tubs is only meant where there is a perfect Necessity, and Tubs and Room enough can't be had to lay the wort thin.

By this Method of Brewing, Ale may be made as strong or as small as is thought fit, and so may the small Beer that comes after, and is so agreeable that this Brewer makes his Ale and strong keeping *October* Beer, all one and the same way, only with this Difference, that the latter is stronger and more hopp'd than the former. Where little or no small Beer is wanted, there may little or none be Brewed, according to this manner of Working, which is no small Conveniency to a little Family that uses more strong than small, nor is there any Loss by leaving the Grainy in some Heart, where Horse, Cows, Hogs, or Rabbits are kept.

I am very sensible that the Vulgar Error for many Years, has been a standard Sign to the ignorant of boiling strong Worts only till they break or curdle in the Copper, which sometimes will be in three quarters of an Hour, or in an Hour or more, according to the nature of the Malt and Water; but from these in some measure I dissent, and also from those that boil it two or three Hours, for it is certain the longer worts boil, the thicker they are made, because the watry or thin parts evaporate first away, and the thicker any Drink is boiled, the longer it requires to lye in the Barrel to have its Particles broke, which Age must be then the sole cause of, and therefore I have fixed the time and sign to know when the wort is truly enough, and that in such, a manner that an ordinary Capacity may be a true judge of, which hereafter will prevent prodigious Losses in the waste of strong worts that have often been boiled away to greater Loss than Profit.

I have here also made known, I think, the true Method of managing the Hop in the Copper, which has long wanted adjusting, to prevent the great damage that longer boilings of them has been the sole occasion of to the spoiling of most of our malt Drinks brewed in this Nation.

CHAP. X.

The Nature and Use of the Hop.

This Vegetable has suffered its degradation, and raised its Reputation on the most of any other. It formerly being thought an unwholsome Ingredient, and till of late a great breeder of the Stone in the Bladder, but now that falacious Notion is obviated by Dr_.Quincy_ and others, who have proved that Malt Drink much tinctured by the Hop, is less prone to do that mischief, than Ale that has fewer boiled in it. Indeed when the Hop in a dear time is adulterated with water, in which Aloes, etc. have been infused, as was practised it is said about eight Years ago to make the old ones recover their bitterness and seem new, then they are to be looked on as unwholsome; but the pure new Hop is surely of a healthful Nature, composed of a spirituous flowery part, and a phlegmatick terrene part, and with the best of the Hops I can either make or mar the Brewing, for if the Hops are boiled in strong or small worts beyond their fine and pure Nature, the Liquor suffers, and will be tang'd with a noxious taste both ungrateful and unwholsome to the Stomach, and if boiled to a very great Excess, they will be apt to cause Reachings and disturb a weak Constitution. It is for these Reasons that I advise the boiling two Parcels of fresh Hops in each Copper of Ale-wort, and if there were three for keeping Beer, it would be so much the better for the taste, health of Body and longer Preservation of the Beer in a sound smooth Condition. And according to this, one of my Neighbours made a Bag like a Pillow-bear of the ordinary sixpenny yard Cloth, and boil'd his Hops in it half an Hour, then he took them out, and put in another Bag of the like quantity of fresh Hops and boiled them half an Hour more, by which means he had an opportunity of boiling both Wort and Hops their due time, sav'd himself the trouble of draining them thro' a Sieve, and secured the Seeds of the Hops at the same time from mixing with the Drink, afterwards he boiled the same Bags in his small Beer till he got the goodness of it out, but observe that the Bags were made bigger than what would just contain the Hops, otherwise it will be difficult to boil out their goodness. It's true, that here is a Charge encreased by the Consumption of a greater quantity of Hops than usual, but then how greatly will they answer the desired end of enjoying fine palated wholsome Drink, that in a cheap time will not amount to much if bought at the best Hand; and if we consider their after-use and benefit in small Beer, there is not any loss at all in their Quantity: But where it can be afforded, the very small Beer would be much improved if fresh Hops were also shifted in the boiling of this as well as the stronger worts, and then it would be neighbourly Charity to give them away to the poorer Person. Hence may appear the Hardship that many are under of being necessitated to drink of those Brewers Malt Liquors, who out of avarice boil their Hops to the last, that they may not lose any of their quintessence: Nay, I have known some of the little Victualling Brewers so stupendiously ignorant, that they have thought they acted the good Husband, when they have squeezed the Hops after they have been boiled to the last in small Beer, to get out all their goodness as they vainly imagin'd, which is so reverse to good management, that in my Opinion they had much better put some sort of Earth into the Drink, and it would prove more pleasant and wholsome. And why the small Beer should be in this manner (as I may justly call it) spoiled for want of the trifling Charge of a few fresh Hops, I am a little surprized at, since is the most general Liquor of Families and therefore as great Care is due to as any in its Brewing, to enjoy it in pure and wholsome Order.

After the Wort is cooled and put into the working Vat or Tub, some have thrown fresh Hops into it, and worked them with the Yeast, at the same time reserving a few Gallons of raw Wort to wash the Yeast thro' a Sieve to keep back the Hop.

This is a good way when Hops enough have not been sufficiently boiled in the Wort, or to preserve it in the Coolers where it is laid thick, otherwise I think it needless.

When Hops have been dear, many have used the Seeds of Wormwood, the they buy in the London Seed Shops instead of them: Others *Daucus* or wild Carrot Seed, that grows in our common Fields, which many of the poor People in this Country gather and dry in their Houses against their wanting of them: Others that wholsome Herb *Horehound*, which indeed is a fine Bitter and grows on several of our Commons.

But before I conclude this Article, I shall take notice of a Country Bite, as I have already done of a *London* one, and that is, of an Arch Fellow that went about to Brew for People, and took his opportunity to save all the used Hops that were to be thrown away, these he washed clean, then would dry them in the Sun, or by the Fire, and sprinkle the juice of *Horehound* on them, which would give them such a greenish colour and bitterish taste, that with the help of the Screw-press he would sell them for new Hops.

Hops in themselves are known to be a subtil grateful Bitter, whose Particles are Active and Rigid, by which the viscid ramous parts of the Malt are much divided, that makes the Drink easy of Digestion in the Body; they also keep it from running into such Cohesions as would make it ropy, valid and sour, and therefore are not only of great use in boiled, but in raw worts to preserve them sound till they can be put into the Copper, and afterwards in the Tun while the Drink is working, as I have before hinted.

Here then I must observe, that the worser earthy part of the Hop is greatly the cause of that rough, harsh unpleasant taste, which accompany both Ales and Beers that have the Hops so long boiled in them as to tincture their worts with their, mischievous Effects; for notwithstanding the Malt, be ever so good, the Hops, if boiled too long in them, will be so predominant as to cause a nasty bad taste, and therefore I am in hopes our Malt Liquors in general will be in great Perfection, when Hops are made use of according to my Directions, and also that more Grounds will be planted with this most serviceable Vegetable than ever, that their Dearness may not be a disencouragement to this excellent Practice.

For I know an Alehouse keeper and Brewer, who, to save the expence of Hops that were then two Shillings *per* Pound, use but a quartern instead of a Pound, the rest he supplied with *Daucus* Seeds; but to be more particular, in a Mug of this Person's Ale I discovered three several Impositions. *First*, He underboil'd his Wort to save its Consumption: *Secondly*, He boiled this Seed instead of the Hop; and *Thirdly*, He beat the Yeast in for some time to encrease the strength of the Drink; and all these in such a *Legerdemain* manner as gull'd and infatuated the ignorant Drinker to such a degree as not to suspect the Fraud, and that for these three Reasons: *First*, The underboil'd wort being of a more sweet taste than ordinary, was esteemed the Produce of a great allowance of Malt. *Secondly*, The *Daucus* Seed encreased their approbation by the fine Peach flavour or relish that it gives the Drink; and *Thirdly*, The Yeast was not so much as thought of, since they enjoyed a strong heady Liquor. These artificial Qualities, and I think I may say unnatural, has been so prevalent with the Vulgar, who were his chief Customers, that I have known this Victualler have more Trade for such Drink than his Neighours, who had much more wholsome at the same time; for the *Daucus* Seed tho' it is a Carminative, and has some other good Properties, yet in the unboil'd Wort it is not capable of doing the Office of the Hop, in breaking thro' the clammy parts of it; the Hop being full of subtil penetrating Qualities, a Strengthener of the Stomach, and makes the Drink agreeble, by opposing Obstructions of the *Viscera*, and particularly of the Liver and Kidneys, as the Learned maintain, which confutes the old Notion, that Hops are a Breeder of the Stone in the Bladder.

CHAP. XI.

Of Boiling Malt Liquors.

Altho' I have said an Hour and a half is requisite for boiling *October* Beer, and an Hour for Ales and small Beer; yet it is to be observed, that an exact time is not altogether a certain Rule in this Case with some Brewers; for when loose Hops are boiled in the wort so long till they all sink, their Seeds will arise and fall down again; the wort also will be curdled, and broke into small Particles if examin'd in a Hand-bowl, but afterwards into larger, as big as great Pins heads, and will appear clean and fine at the Top. This is so much a Rule with some, that they regard not Time but this Sign to shew when the Wort is boiled enough; and this will happen sooner or later according to the Nature of the Barley and its being well Malted; for if it comes off Chalks or Gravels, it generally has the good Property of breaking or curdling soon; but if of tough Clays, then it is longer, which by some Persons is not a little valued, because it saves time in boiling, and consequently the Consumption of the Wort.

It is also to be observed, that pale Malt Worts will not break so soon in the Copper, as the brown Sorts, but when either of their Worts boil, it should be to the purpose, for then they will break sooner and waste less than if they are kept Simmering, and will likewise work more kindly in the Tun, drink smoother, and keep longer.

Now all Malt Worts may be spoiled by too little or too much boiling; if too little, then the Drink will always taste raw, mawkish, and be unwholsome in the Stomach, where, instead of helping to dilute and digest our Food, it will cause Obstructions, Colicks, Head-achs, and other misfortunes; besides, all such underboil'd Drinks are certainly exposed to staleness and sowerness, much sooner than those that have had their full time in the Copper. And if they are boiled too long, they will then thicken (for one may boil a Wort to a Salve) and not come out of the Copper fine and in a right Condition, which will cause it never to be right clear in the Barrel; an *Item* sufficient to shew the mistake of all those that think to excel in Malt Liquors, by boiling them two or three Hours, to the great Confusion of the Wort, and doing more harm than good to the Drink.

But to be more particular in those two Extreams, it is my Opinion, as I have said before, that no Ale Worts boiled less than an Hour can be good, because in an Hour's time they cannot acquire a thickness of Body any ways detrimental to them, and in less than an Hour the ramous viscid parts of the Ale cannot be sufficiently broke and divided, so as to prevent it running into Cohesions, Ropyness and Sowerness, because in Ales there are not Hops enough allowed to do this, which good boiling must in a great measure supply, or else such Drink I am sure can never be agreeable to the Body of Man; for then its cohesive Parts being not thoroughly broke and comminuted by time and boiling, remains in a hard texture of Parts, which consequently obliges the Stomach to work more than ordinary to digest and secrete such parboiled Liquor, that time and fire should have cured before: Is not this apparent in half boil'd Meats, or under-bak'd Bread, that often causes the Stomach a great fatigue to digest, especially in those of a sedentary Life; and if that suffers, 'tis certain the whole Body must share in it: How ignorant then are those People, who, in tipling of such Liquor, can praise it for excellent good Ale, as I have been an eye-witness of, and only because its taste is sweetish, (which is the nature of such raw Drinks) as believing it to be the pure Effects of the genuine Malt, not perceiving the Landlord's Avarice and Cunning to save the Consumption of his Wort by shortness of boiling, tho' to the great Prejudice of the Drinker's Health; and because a Liquid does not afford such a plain ocular Demonstration, as Meat and Bread does, these deluded People are taken into an Approbation of indeed an *Ignis fatuus*, or what is not.

To come then to the *Crisis* of the Matter, both Time and the Curdling or Breaking of the Wort should be consulted; for if a Person was to boil the Wort an Hour, and then take it out of the Copper, before it was rightly broke, it would be wrong management, and the Drink would not be fine nor wholsome; and if it should boil an Hour and a half, or two Hours, without regarding when its Particles are in a right order, then it may be too thick, so that due Care must be had to the two extreams to obtain it its due order; therefore in *October* and keeping Beers, an Hour and a quarter's good boiling is commonly sufficient to have a thorough cured Drink, for generally in that time it will break and boil enough, and because in this there is a double Security by length of boiling, and a quantity of Hops shifted; but in the new way there is only a single one, and that is by a double or treble allowance of fresh Hops boiled only half an Hour in the Wort, and for this Practice a Reason is assigned, that the Hops being endowed with discutient aperitive Qualities, will by them and their great quantity supply the Defect of underboiling the Wort; and that a further Conveniency is here enjoyed by having only the fine wholsome strong flowery spirituous Parts of the Hop in the Drink, exclusive of the phlegmatick nasty earthy Parts which would be extracted if the Hops were to be boiled above half an Hour; and therefore there are many now, that are so attach'd to this new Method, that they won't brew Ale or *October* Beer any other way, vouching it to be a true Tenet, that if Hops are boiled above thirty Minutes, the wort will have some or more of their worser Quality. The allowance of Hops for Ale or Beer, cannot be exactly adjusted without coming to Particulars, because the Proportion should be according to the nature and

29

quality of the Malt, the Season of the Year it is brew'd in, and the length of time it is to be kept.

For strong brown Ale brew'd in any of the Winter Months, and boiled an Hour, one Pound is but barely sufficient for a Hogshead, if it be Tapp'd in three Weeks or a Month.

If for pale Ale brewed at that time and for that Age, one Pound and a quarter of Hops; but if these Ales are brewed in any of the Summer Months, there should be more Hops allowed.

For *October* or *March* brown Beer, a Hogshead made from Eleven Bushels of Malt, boiled an Hour and a quarter to be kept Nine Months, three Pounds and a half ought to be boiled in such Drink at the least.

For *October* or *March*, pale Beer made from fourteen Bushels, boiled an Hour and a quarter, and kept Twelve Months, six Pound ought to be allowed to a Hogshead of such Drink, and more if the Hops are shifted in two Bags, and less time given the Wort to boil.

Now those that are of Opinion, that their Beer and Ales are greatly improved by boiling the Hops only half an Hour in the Wort, I joyn in Sentiment with them, as being very sure by repeated Experience it is so; but I must here take leave to dissent from those that think that half an Hour's boiling the Wort is full enough for making right sound and well relished Malt Drinks; however of this I have amply and more particularly wrote in my Second Book of Brewing in Chapter IV, where I have plainly publish'd the true Sign or Criterion to know when the Wort is boiled just enough, and which I intend to publish in a little time.

CHAP. XII.

Of Foxing or Tainting Malt Liquors.

Foxing is a misfortune, or rather a Disease in Malt Drinks, occasioned by divers Means, as the Nastiness of the Utensils, putting the Worts too thick together in the Backs or Cooler, Brewing too often and soon one after another, and sometimes by bad Malts and Waters, and the Liquors taken in wrong Heats, being of such pernicious Consequence to the great Brewer in particular, that he sometimes cannot recover and bring his Matters into a right Order again under a Week or two, and is so hateful to him in its very Name, that it is a general Law among them to make all Servants that Name the word *Fox* or *Foxing*, in the Brewhouse to pay Sixpence, which obliges them to call it *Reynards*; for when once the Drink is Tainted, it may be smelt at some Distance somewhat like a *Fox*; It chiefly happens in hot weather, and causes the Beer and Ale so Tainted to acquire a fulsome sickish taste, that will if it is receive'd in a great degree become Ropy like Treacle, and in some short time turn Sour. This I have known so to surprize my small Beer Customers, that they have asked the Drayman what was the matter: He to act in his Master's Interest tells them a Lye, and says it is the goodness of the Malt that causes that sweetish mawkish taste, and then would brag at Home how cleverly he came off. I have had it also in the Country more than once, and that by the idleness and ignorance of my Servant, who when a Tub has been rinced out only with fair Water, has set it by for a clean one but this won't do with a careful Master for I oblige him to clean the Tub with a Hand-brush, Ashes, or Sand every Brewing, and so that I cannot scrape any Dirt up under my Nail. However as the Cure of this Disease has baffled the Efforts of many, I have been tempted to endeavour the finding out a Remedy for the great Malignity, and shall deliver the best I know on this Score.

And here I shall mention the great Value of the Hop in preventing and curing the Fox in Malt Liquors. When the Wort is run into the Tub out of the mashing Vat, it is a very good way to throw some Hops directly into it before it is put into the Copper, and they will secure it against Sourness and Ropyness, that are the two Effects of fox'd Worts or Drinks, and is of such Power in this respect, that raw Worts may be kept some time, even, in hot weather, before they are boiled, and which is necessary; where there is a large Quantity of Malt used to a little Copper; but it is certain that the stronger Worts will keep longer with Hops than the smaller Sorts: So likewise if a Person has fewer Tubs than is wanting, and he is apprehensive his Worts will be Fox'd by too thick lying in the Coolers or working Tubs, then it will be a safe way to put some fresh Hops into such Tubs and work them with the Yeast as I have before hinted; or in case the Drink is already Foxed in the Fat or Tun, new Hops should be put in and work'd with it, and they will greatly fetch it again into a right Order; but then such Drink should be carefully taken clear off from its gross nasty Lee, which being mostly Tainted, would otherwise lye in the Barrel, corrupt and make it worse.

Some will sift quick Lime into foxed Drinks while they are working in the Tun or Vat, that its Fire and Salts may break the Cohesions of the Beer or Ale, and burn away the stench, that the Corruption would always cause; but then such Drink should by a Peg at the bottom of the Vat be drawn off as fine as possible, and the Dregs left behind.

There are many that do not conceive how their Drinks become Fox'd and Tainted for several Brewings together; but I have in Chapter VI, in my Second Book, made it appear, that the Taint is chiefly retain'd and lodged in the upright wooden Pins that fasten the Planks to the Joists, and how scalding Lye is a very efficacious Liquor to extirpate it out of the Utensils in a little time if rightly applied; and one other most powerful Ingredient that is now used by the greatest Artists for curing of the same.

CHAP. XIII

Of fermenting and working of Beers and Ales, and the pernicious Practice of Beating in the Yeast detected.

This Subject in my Opinion has, long wanted a Satyrical Pen to shew the ill Effects of this unwholsome Method, which I suppose has been much discouraged and hindered hitherto, from the general use it has been under many Years, especially by the *Northern* Brewers, who tho' much famed for their Knowledge in this Art, and have induced many others by their Example in the *Southern* and other Parts to pursue their Method; yet I shall endeavour to prove them culpable of Male-practice, that beat in the Yeast, as some of them have done a Week together; and that Custom ought not to Authorize an ill Practice. *First*, I shall observe that Yeast is a very strong acid, that abounds with subtil spirituous Qualities, whose Particles being wrapped up in those that are viscid, are by a mixture with them in the Wort, brought into an intestine Motion, occasion'd by Particles of different Gravities; for as the spirituous Parts of the Wort will be continually striving to get up to the Surface, the glutinous adhesive ones of the Yeast will be as constant in retarding their assent, and so prevent their Escape; by which the spirituous Particles are set loose and free from their viscid Confinements, as may appear by the Froth on the Top, and to this end a moderate warmth hastens the Operation, as it assists in opening the viscidities in which some spirituous Parts may be entangled, and unbends the Spring of the included Air: The viscid Parts which are raised to the Top, not only on account of their own lightness, but by the continual efforts and occursions of the Spirits to get uppermost, shew when the ferment is at the highest, and prevent the finer Spirits making their escape; but if this intestine Operation is permitted to continue too long, a great deal will get away, and the remaining grow flat and vapid, as Dr. *Quincy* well observes. Now tho' a small quantity of Yeast is necessary to break the Band of Corruption in the Wort, yet it is in itself of a poisonous Nature, as many other Acids are; for if a Plaister of thick Yeast be applied to the Wrist as some have done for an Ague, it will there raise little Pustules or Blisters in some degree like that Venomous! (As I have just reason in a particular Sense to call it) Ingredient *Cantharide*, which is one of the Shop Poisons. Here then I shall observe, that I have known several beat the Yeast into the Wort for a Week or more together to improve it, or in plainer terms to load the Wort with its weighty and strong spirituous Particles; and that for two Reasons, *First*, Because it will make the Liquor so heady, that five Bushels of Malt may be equal in strength to six, and that by the stupifying Narcotick Qualities of the Yeast; which mercenary subtilty and imposition has so prevailed to my Knowledge with the Vulgar and Ignorant, that it has caused many of them to return the next Day to the same Alehouse, as believing they had stronger and better Drink than others: But alas, how are such deceived that know no other than that it is the pure Product of the Malt, when at the same time they are driving Nails into their Coffins, by impregnating their Blood with the corrupt Qualities of this poisonous acid, as many of its Drinkers have proved, by suffering violent Head-achs, loss of Appetite, and other Inconveniencies the Day following, and sometimes longer, after a Debauch of such Liquor; who would not perhaps for a great reward swallow a Spoonful of thick Yeast by itself, and yet without any concern may receive for ought they know several, dissolved in the Vehicle of Ale, and then the corrosive Corpuscles of the Yeast being mix'd with the Ale, cannot fail (when forsaken in the Canals of the Body of their Vehicle) to do the same mischief as they would if taken by themselves undiluted, only with this difference, that they may in this Form be carried sometimes further in the animal

32

Frame, and so discover their malignity in some of the inmost recesses thereof, which also is the very Case of malignant Waters, as a most learned Doctor observes.

Secondly, They alledge for beating the Yeast into Wort, that it gives it a fine tang or relish, or as they call it at *London*, it makes the Ale bite of the Yeast; but this flourish indeed is for no other reason than to further its Sale, and tho' it may be agreeable to some Bigots, to me it proves a discovery of the infection by its nauseous taste; however my surprize is lessen'd, when I remember the *Plymouth* People, who are quite the reverse of them at *Dover* and *Chatham*; for the first are so attach'd to their white thick Ale, that many have undone themselves by drinking it; nor is their humour much different as to the common Brewers brown Ale, who when the Customer wants a Hogshead, they immediately put in a Handful of Salt and another of Flower, and so bring it up, this is no sooner on the Stilling but often Tapp'd, that it may carry a Froth on the Top of the Pot, otherwise they despise it: The Salt commonly answered its End of causing the Tiplers to become dryer by the great Quantities they drank, that it farther excited by the biting pleasant stimulating quality the Salt strikes the Palate with. The Flower also had its seducing share by pleasing the Eye and Mouth with its mantling Froth, so that the Sailors that are often here in great Numbers used to consume many Hogsheads of this common Ale with much delight, as thinking it was intirely the pure Product of the Malt.

Their white Ale is a clear Wort made from pale Malt, and fermented with what they call ripening, which is a Composition, they say, of the Flower of Malt, Yeast and Whites of Eggs, a *Nostrum* made and sold only by two or three in those Parts, but the Wort is brewed and the Ale vended by many of the Publicans; which is drank while it is fermenting in Earthen Steens, in such a thick manner as resembles butter'd Ale, and sold for Twopence Halfpenny the full Quart. It is often prescribed by Physicians to be drank by wet Nurses for the encrease of their Milk, and also as a prevalent Medicine for the Colick and Gravel. But the *Dover* and *Chatham* People won't drink their Butt-Beer, unless it is Aged, fine and strong.

Of working and fermenting London *Stout Beer and Ale.*

In my Brewhouse at *London*, the Yeast at once was put into the Tun to work the Stout Beer and Ale with, as not having the Conveniency of doing otherwise, by reason the After-worts of small Beer comes into the same Backs or Coolers where the strong Worts had just been, by this means, and the shortness of time we have to ferment our strong Drinks, we cannot make Reserves of cold Worts to mix with and check the too forward working of those Liquors, for there we brewed three times a Week throughout the Year, as most of the great ones do in *London*, and some others five times. The strong Beer brewed for keeping is suffered to be Blood-warm in the Winter when the Yeast is put into it, that it may gradually work two Nights and a Day at least, for this won't admit of such a hasty Operation as the common brown Ale will, because if it is work'd too warm and hasty, such Beer won't keep near so long as that fermented cooler. The brown Ale

33

has indeed its Yeast put into it in the Evening very warm, because they carry it away the very next Morning early to their Customers, who commonly draw it out in less than a Week's time. The Pale or Amber Ales are often kept near it, not quite a Week under a fermentation, for the better incorporating the Yeast with Wort, by beating it in several times for the foregoing Reasons.

Of working or fermenting Drinks brewed by Private Families.

I mean such who Brew only for their own use, whether it be a private Family or a Victualler. In this Case be it for Stout Beers, or for any of the Ales; the way that is used in *Northamptonshire,* and by good Brewers elsewhere; is, to put some Yeast into a small quantity of warm Wort in a Hand-bowl, which for a little while swims on the Top, where it works out and leisurely mixes with the Wort, that is first quite cold in Summer, and almost so in Winter; for the cooler it is work'd the longer it will keep, too much Heat agitating the spirituous Particles into too quick a motion, whereby they spend themselves too fast, or fly away too soon, and then the Drink will certainly work into a blister'd Head that is never natural; but when it ferments by moderate degrees into a fine white curl'd Head, its Operation is then truly genuine, and plainly shews the right management of the Brewer. To one Hogshead of Beer, that is to be kept nine Months, I put a Quart of thick Yeast, and ferment it as cool as it will admit of, two Days together, in *October* or *March,* and if I find it works too fast, I check it at leisure by stirring in some raw Wort with a Hand-bowl: So likewise in our Country Ales we take the very same method, because of having them keep some time, and this is so nicely observed by several, that I have seen them do the very same by their small Beer Wort; now by these several Additions of raw Wort, there are as often new Commotions raised in the Beer or Ale, which cannot but contribute to the rarefaction and comminution of the whole; but whether it is by these joining Principles of the Wort and Yeast, that the Drink is rendered smoother, or that the spirituous Parts are more entangled and kept from making their Escape, I can't determine; yet sure it is, that such small Liquors generally sparkle and knit out of the Barrel as others out of a Bottle, and is as pleasant Ale as ever I drank.

Others again for Butt or Stout Beer will, when they find it works up towards a thick Yeast, mix it once and beat it in again with the Hand-bowl or Jett; and when it has work'd up a second time in such a manner, they put it into the Vessel with the Yeast on the Top and the Sediments at Bottom, taking particular Care to have some more in a Tub near the Cask to fill it up as it works over, and when it has done working, leave it with a thick Head of Yeast on to preserve it.

But for Ale that is not to be kept very long, they Hop it accordingly, and beat the Yeast in every four or five Hours for two Days successively in the warm weather, and four in the Winter till the Yeast begins to work heavy and sticks to the hollow part of the Bowl, if turned down on the same, then they take all the Yeast off at Top and leave all the Dregs behind, putting only up the clear Drink, and when it is a little work'd in the Barrel, it will be fine in a few Days and ready for drinking. But this, last way of beating in the Yeast too long, I think I have sufficiently detected, and hope, as it is how declining, it will never revive again, and for which reason I have in my second Book encouraged all light fermentations, as the most natural for the Malt Liquor and the human Body.

Of forwarding and retarding the fermentation of malt Liquors.

In case Beer or Ale is backward in working, it is often practised to cast some Flower out of the Dusting Box, or with the Hand over the Top of the Drink, which will become a sort of Crust or Cover to help to keep the Cold out: Others will put in one or two Ounces of powder'd Ginger, which will so heat the Wort as to bring it forward: Others will take a Gallon Stone Bottle and fill it with boiling water, which being well Cork'd, is put into the working Tub, where it will communicate a gradual Heat for some time and forward the fermentation: Others will reserve some raw Wort, which they heat and mix with the rest, but then due Care must be taken that the Pot in which it is heated has no manner of Grease about it lest it impedes, instead of promoting the working, and for this reason some nice Brewers will not suffer a Candle too near the Wort, lest it drop into it. But for retarding and keeping back any Drink that is too much heated in working, the cold raw Wort, as I have said before, is the most proper of any thing to check it with, tho' I have known some to put one or more Pewter Dishes into it for that purpose, or it may be broke into several other Tubs, where by its shallow lying it will be taken off its Fury. Others again, to make Drink work that is backward, will take the whites of two Eggs and beat them up with half a Quartern of good Brandy, and put it either into the working Vat, or into the Cask, and it will quickly bring it forward if a warm Cloth is put over the Bung. Others will tye up Bran in a coarse thin Cloth and put it into the Vat, where by its spungy and flowery Nature and close Bulk it will absorp a quantity of the Drink, and breed a heat to forward its working. I know an Inn-keeper of a great Town in *Bucks* that is so curious as to take off all the top Yeast first, and then by a Peg near the bottom of his working Tub, he draws off the Beer or Ale, so that the Dreggs are by this means left behind. This I must own is very right in Ales that are to be drank soon, but in Beers that are to lye nine or twelve Months in a Butt or other Cask, there certainly will be wanted some Feces or Sediment for the Beer to feed on, else it must consequently grow hungry, sharp and eager; and therefore if its own top and bottom are not put into a Cask with the Beer, some other Artificial Composition or Lee should supply its Place, that is wholsomer, and will better feed with such Drink than its own natural Settlement, and therefore I have here inserted several curious Receipts for answering this great End.

CHAP. XIV.

Of an Artificial Lee for Stout or Stale Beer to feed on.

This Article, as it is of very great Importance in the curing of our malt Liquors, requires a particular regard to this last management of them, because in my Opinion the general misfortune of the Butt or keeping Beers drinking so hard and harsh, is partly owing to the nasty foul Feces that lye at the bottom of the Cask, compounded of the Sediments of Malt, Hops and Yeast, that are, all

Clogg'd with gross rigid Salts, which by their long lying in the Butt or other Vessel, so tinctures the Beer as to make it partake of all their raw Natures: For such is the Feed, such is the Body, as may be perceived by Eels taken out of dirty Bottoms, that are sure to have a muddy taste, when the Silver sort that are catched in Gravelly or Sandy clear Rivers Eat sweet and fine: Nor can this ill property be a little in those Starting (as they call it in *London*) new thick Beers that were carry'd directly from my Brewhouse, and by a Leather Pipe or Spout conveyed into the Butt as they stood in the Cellar, which I shall further demonstrate by the Example of whole Wheat, that is, by many put into such Beer to feed and preserve it, as being reckoned a substantial Alcali; however it has been proved that such Wheat in about three Years time has eat into the very Wood of the Cask, and there Hony-comb'd it by making little hollow Cavities in the Staves. Others there are that will hang a Bag of Wheat in the Vessel that it mayn't touch the Bottom, but in both Cases the Wheat is discovered to absorp and collect the saline acid qualities of the Beer, Yeast and Hop, by which it is impregnated with their sharp qualities, as a Toast of Bread is put into Punch or Beer, whose alcalous hollow Nature will attract and make a Lodgment of the acid strong Particles in either, as is proved by eating the inebriating Toast, and therefore the *Frenchman* says, the *English* are right in putting a Toast into the Liquor, but are Fools for eating it: Hence it is that such whole Wheat is loaded with the qualities of the unwholsome Settlements or Grounds of the Beer, and becomes of such a corroding Nature, as to do this mischief; and for that reason, some in the *North* will hang a Bag of the Flower of malted Oats, Wheat, Pease and Beans in the Vessels of Beer, as being a lighter and mellower Body than whole Wheat or its Flower, and more natural to the Liquor: But whether it be raw Wheat or Malted, it is supposed, after this receptacle has emitted its alcalous Properties to the Beer, and taken in all it can of the acid qualities thereof, that such Beer will by length of Age prey upon that again, and so communicate its pernicious Effects to the Body of Man, as Experience seems to justify by the many sad Examples that I have seen in the Destruction of several lusty Brewers Servants, who formerly scorn'd what they then called Flux Ale, to the preference of such corroding consuming Stale Beers; and therefore I have hereafter advised that such Butt or keeping Beers be Tapp'd at nine or twelve Months end at furthest, and then an Artificial Lee will have a due time allowed it to do good and not harm.

An Excellent Composition for feeding Butts or keeping Beers with.

Take a Quart of *French* Brandy, or as much of *English*, that is free from any burnt Tang, or other ill taste, and is full Proof, to this put as much Wheat or Flower as will knead it into a Dough, put it in long pieces into the Bung Hole, as soon as the Beer has done working, or afterwards, and let it gently fall piece by piece to the bottom of the Butt, this will maintain the Drink in a mellow freshness, keep staleness off for some time, and cause it to be the stronger as it grows Aged.

ANOTHER.

Take one Pound of Treacle or Honey, one Pound of the Powder of dryed Oyster-shells or fat Chalk, mix them well and put it into a Butt, as soon as it has done working or some time after, and Bung it well, this will both fine and preserve the Beer in a soft, smooth Condition for a great while.

ANOTHER.

Take a Peck of Egg-shells and dry them in an Oven, break and mix them with two Pound of fat Chalk, and mix them with water wherein four Pounds of coarse Sugar has been boiled, and put it into the Butt as aforesaid.

To fine and preserve Beers and Ales by boiling an Ingredient in the Wort.

This most valuable way I frequently follow both for Ale, Butt-beer and Small Beer, and that is, in each Barrel Copper of Wort, I put in a Pottle, or two Quarts of whole Wheat as soon as I can, that it may soak before it boils, then I strain it thro' a Sieve, when I put the Wort in cooling Tubs, and if it is thought fit the same Wheat may be boiled in a second Copper: Thus there will be extracted a gluey Consistence, which being incorporated with the Wort by boiling, gives it a more thick and ponderous Body, and when in the Cask, soon makes a Sediment or Lee, as the Wort is more or less loaded with the weighty Particles of this fizy Body; but if such Wheat was first parched or baked in an Oven, it would do better, as being rather too raw as it comes from the Ear.

Another Way.

A Woman, who lived at *Leighton Buzzard* in *Bedfordshire,* and had the best Ale in the Town, once told a Gentleman, she had Drink just done working in the Barrel, and before it was Bung'd would wager it was fine enough to Drink out of a Glass, in which it should maintain a little while a high Froth; and it was true, for the Ivory shavings that she boiled in her Wort, was the Cause of it, which an Acquaintance of mine accidentally had a View of as they lay spread over the Wort in the Copper; so will Hartshorn shavings do the same and better, both of them being great finers and preservers of malt Liquors against staleness and sourness, and are certainly of a very alcalous Nature. Or if they are put into a Cask when you Bung it down, it will be of service for that purpose; but these are dear in Comparison of the whole Wheat, which will in a great measure supply their Place, and after it is used, may be given to a poor Body, or to the Hog.

To stop the Fret in Malt Liquors.

Take a Quart of Black Cherry Brandy, and pour it in at the Bung-hole of the Hogshead and stop it close.

To recover deadish Beer.

When strong Drink grows flat, by the loss of its Spirits, take four or five Gallons out of a Hogshead, and boil it with five Pound of Honey, skim it, and when cold, put it to the rest, and stop it up close: This will make it pleasant, quick and strong.

To make stale Beer drink new.

Take the Herb *Horehound* stamp it and strain it, then put a Spoonful of the juice (which is an extream good Pectoral) to a pitcher-full of Beer, let it stand covered about two Hours and drink it.

To fine Malt Liquors.

Take a pint of water, half an Ounce of unslack'd Lime, mix them well together, let it stand three Hours and the Lime will settle to the Bottom, and the water be as clear as Glass, pour the water from the Sediment, and put it into your Ale or Beer, mix it with half an Ounce of Ising-glass first cut small and boiled, and in five Hours time or less the Beer in the Barrel will settle and clear.

There are several other Compositions that may be used for this purpose, but none that I ever heard of will answer like those most Excellent Balls that Mr. *Ellis* of *Little Gaddesden* in *Hertfordshire* has found out by his own Experience to be very great Refiners, Preservers and Relishers of Malt Liquors and Cyders, and will also recover damag'd Drinks, as I have mentioned in my Second Book, where I have given a further Account of some other things that will fine, colour and improve Malt Drinks: The Balls are sold at [missing text]

CHAP. XV.

Of several pernicious Ingredients put into Malt Liquors to encrease their Strength.

Malt Liquors, as well as several others, have long lain under the disreputation of being adulterated and greatly abused by avaricious and ill-principled People, to augment their Profits at the Expence of the precious Health of human Bodies, which, tho' the greatest Jewel in Life, is said to be too often lost by the Deceit of the Brewer, and the Intemperance of the Drinker: This undoubtedly was one, and I believe the greatest, of the Lord *Bacon's* Reasons for saying, he thought not one *Englishman* in a thousand died a natural Death. Nor is it indeed to be much wondered at, when, according to Report, several of the Publicans make it their Business to study and practise this Art, witness what I am afraid is too true, that some have made use of the *Coculus India* Berry for making Drink heady, and saving the Expence of Malt; but as this is a violent Potion by its narcotick stupifying Quality, if taken in too large a degree, I hope this will be rather a prevention of its use than an invitation, it being so much of the nature of the deadly Nightshade, that it bears the same Character; and I am sure the latter is bad enough; for one of my Neighbour's Brothers was killed by eating its Berries that grow in some of our Hedges, and so neatly resembles the black Cherry, that the Boy took the wrong for the right.

There is another sinister Practice said to be frequently used by ill Persons to supply the full quantity of Malt, and that is *Coriander* Seeds: This also is of a heady nature boiled in the Wort, one Pound of which will answer to a Bushel of

Malt, as was ingenuously confess'd to me by a Gardener, who own'd he sold a great deal of it to Alehouse Brewers (for I don't suppose the great Brewer would be concern'd in any such Affair) for that purpose, purpose, at Ten-pence per Pound; but how wretchedly ignorant are those that make use of it, not knowing the way first to cure and prepare it for this and other mixtures, without which it is a dangerous thing, and will cause Sickness in the Drinkers of it. Others are said to make use of Lime-stones to fine and preserve the Drink; but to come off the fairest in such foul Artifices, it has been too much a general Practice to beat the Yeast so long into the Ale, that without doubt it has done great Prejudice to the Healths of many others besides the Person I have writ of in the Preface of my Second Book. For the sake then of Seller and Buyer, I have here offered several valuable Receipts for fining, preserving and mellowing Beers and Ales, in such a true healthful and beneficial manner, that from henceforth after the Perusal of this Book, and the knowledge of their worth are fully known, no Person, I hope, will be so sordidly obstinate as to have any thing to do with such unwholsome Ingredients; because these are not only of the cheapest sort, but will answer their End and Purpose; and the rather, since Malts are now only twenty Shillings per Quarter, and like to hold a low Price for Reasons that I could here assign.

I own, I formerly thought they were too valuable to expose to the Publick by reason of their Cheapness and great Virtues, as being most of them wholsomer than the Malt itself, which is but a corrupted Grain. But, as I hope they will do considerable Service in the World towards having clear salubrious and pleasant Malt Liquors in most private Families and Alehouses, I have my Satisfaction.

CHAP. XVI.

Of the Cellar or Repository for keeping Beers and Ales.

It's certain by long Experience, that the Weather or Air has not only a Power or Influence in Brewings; but also after the Drink is in the Barrel, Hogshead or Butt, in Cellars or other Places, which is often the cause of forwarding or retarding the fineness of Malt Liquors; for if we brew in cold Weather, and the Drink is to stand in a Cellar of Clay, or where Springs rise, or Waters lye or pass through, such a Place by consequence will check the due working of the Drink, chill, flat, deaden and hinder it from becoming fine. So likewise if Beer or Ale is brewed in hot Weather and put into Chalky, Gravelly or Sandy Cellars, and especially if the Windows open to the South, South-East, or South-West, then it is very likely it will not keep long, but be muddy and stale: Therefore, to keep Beer in such a Cellar, it should be brewed in *October*, that the Drink may have time to cure itself before the hot Weather comes on; but in wettish or damp Cellars, 'tis best to Brew in *March*, that the Drink may have time to fine and settle before the Winter Weather is advanced. Now such Cellar Extremities should, if it could be done, be brought into a temperate State, for which purpose some have been so curious as to have double or treble Doors to their Cellar to keep the Air out, and then carefully shut the outward, before they enter the inward one, whereby it will be more secure from aerial Alterations; for in Cellars and Places, that are most exposed to such Seasons, Malt Liquors are frequently disturb'd and made unfit for a nice Drinker; therefore if a Cellar is kept dry and these Doors to it, it is reckoned warm in Winter and cool in Summer, but the best of Cellars are thought to be those in Chalks, Gravels or Sands, and particularly in Chalks, which are of a drying quality more than any other, and consequently dissipates Damps the most of all Earths, which makes it contribute much to the good keeping of the Drink; for all damp Cellars are prejudicial to the Preservation of Beers and Ales, and sooner bring on the rotting of the Casks and Hoops than the dry ones; Insomuch that in a chalky Cellar near me, their Ashen broad Hoops have lasted above thirty Years. Besides, in such inclosed Cellars and temperate Air, the Beers and Ales ripen more kindly, are better digested and softned, and drink smoother: But when the Air is in a disproportion by the Cellars letting in Heats and Colds, the Drink will grow Stale and be disturbed, sooner than when the Air is kept out. From hence it is, that in some Places their Malt Liquors are exceeding good, because they brew with Pale or Amber Malts, Chalky Water, and keep their Drinks in close Vaults or proper dry Cellars, which is of such Importance, that notwithstanding any Malt Liquor may be truly brewed, yet it may be spoiled in a bad Cellar that may cause such alternate Fermentations as to make it thick and sour, tho' it sometimes happens that after such Changes it fines itself again; and to prevent these Commotions of the Beer, some brew their pale Malt in *March* and their brown in *October*, for that the pale Malt, having not so many fiery Particles in it as the brown, stands more in need of the Summer's Weather to ripen it, while the brown sort being more hard and dry is better able to defend itself against the Winter Colds that will help to smooth its harsh Particles; yet when they happen to be too violent, Horse-dung should be laid to the Windows as a Fortification against them; but if there were no Lights at all to a Cellar, it would be better.

Some are of Opinion, that *October* is the best of all other Months to brew any sort of Malt in, by reason there are so many cold Months directly follow, that will digest the Drink and make it much excel that Brewed in *March* because such Beer will not want that Care and Watching, as that brewed in *March* absolutely requires, by often taking out and putting in the Vent-peg on Change of Weather; and if it is always left out, then it deadens and palls the Drink; yet if due Care is not taken in this respect, a Thunder or Stormy Night may marr all, by making the Drink ferment and burst the Cask; for which Reason, as Iron Hoops are most in Fashion at this time, they are certainly the greatest Security to the safety of the Drink thus exposed; and next to them is the Chesnut Hoop; both which will endure a shorter or longer time as the Cellar is more or less dry, and the Management attending them. The Iron Hoop generally begins to rust first at the Edges, and therefore should be rubbed off when opportunity offers, and be both kept from wet as much as possible; for 'tis Rust that eats the Iron Hoop in two sometimes in ten or twelve Years, when the Ashen and Chesnut in dry Cellars have lasted three times as long.

CHAP. XVII.

Of Cleaning and Sweetening of Casks.

In Case your Cask is a Butt, then with cold Water first rince out the Lees clean, and have ready, boiling or very hot Water, which put in, and with a long Stale and a little Birch fastened to its End, scrub the Bottom as well as you can. At the same time let there be provided another shorter Broom of about a Foot and a half long, that with one Hand may be so imployed in the upper and other Parts as to clean the Cask well: So in a Hogshead or other smaller Vessel, the one-handed short Broom may be used with Water, or with Water, Sand or Ashes, and be effectually cleaned; the outside of the Cask about the Bung-hole should be well washed, lest the Yeast, as it works over, carries some of its Filth with it.

But to sweeten a Barrel, Kilderkin, Firkin or Pin in the great Brewhouses, they put them over the Copper Hole for a Night together, that the Steam of the boiling Water or Wort may penetrate into the Wood; this Way is such a furious Searcher, that unless the Cask is new hooped just before, it will be apt to fall in pieces.

Another Way.

Take a Pottle, or more, of Stone Lime, and put it into the Cask; on this pour some Water and stop it up directly, shaking it well about.

Another Way.

Take a long Linnen Rag and dip it in melted Brimstone, light it at the end, and let it hang pendant with the upper part of the Rag fastened to the wooden Bung; this is a most quick sure Way, and will not only sweeten, but help to fine the Drink.

Another.

Or to make your Cask more pleasant, you may use the Vintners Way thus: Take four Ounces of Stone Brimstone, one Ounce of burnt Alum, and two Ounces of Brandy; melt all these in an Earthen Pan over hot Coals, and dip therein a piece of new Canvas, and instantly sprinkle thereon the Powders of Nutmegs, Cloves, Coriander and Anise-seeds: This Canvas set on fire, and let it burn hanging in the Cask fastened at the end with the wooden Bung, so that no Smoke comes out.

For a Musty Cask.

Boil some Pepper in water and fill the Cask with it scalding hot.

For a very stinking Vessel.

The last Remedy is the Coopers taking out one of the Heads of the Cask to scrape the inside, or new-shave the Staves, and is the surest way of all others, if it is fired afterwards within-side a small matter, as the Cooper knows how.

These several Methods may be made use of at Discretion, and will be of great Service where they are wanted. The sooner also a Remedy is applied, the better; else the Taint commonly encreases, as many have to their prejudice proved, who have made use of such Casks, in hopes the next Beer will overcome it; but when once a Cask is infected, it will be a long while, if ever, before it becomes sweet, if no Art is used. Many therefore of the careful sort, in case they han't a Convenience to fill their Vessel as soon as it is empty, will stop it close, to prevent the Air and preserve the Lees sound, which will greatly tend to the keeping of the Cask pure and sweet against the next Occasion.

To prepare a new Vessel to keep Malt Liquors in.

A new Vessel is most improperly used by some ignorant People for strong Drink after only once or twice scalding with Water, which is so wrong, that such Beer or Ale will not fail of tasting thereof for half, if not a whole Year afterwards; such is the Tang of the Oak and its Bark, as may be observed from the strong Scents of Tan-Yards, which the Bark is one cause of. To prevent then this Inconvenience, when your Brewing is over put up some Water scalding hot, and let it run throu' the Grains, then boil it and fill up the Cask, stop it well and let it stand till it is cold, do this twice, then take the Grounds of strong Drink and boil in it green Wallnut Leaves and new Hay or Wheat Straw, and put all into the Cask, that it be full and stop it close. After this, use it for small Beer half a Year together, and then it will be thoroughly sweet and fit for strong Drinks; or

Another Way.

Take a new Cask and dig a Hole in the Ground, in which it may lye half depth with the Bung downwards; let it remain a Week, and it will greatly help this or any stinking musty Cask. But besides these, I have writ of two other excellent Ways to sweeten musty or stinking Casks, in my Second Book of Brewing.

Wine Casks.

These, in my Opinion, are the cheapest of all others to furnish a Person readily with, as being many of them good Casks for Malt Liquors, because the Sack and White-Wine sorts are already season'd to Hand, and will greatly improve Beers and Ales that are put in them: But beware of the Rhenish Wine Cask for strong Drinks; for its Wood is so tinctured with this sharp Wine, that it will hardly ever be free of it, and therefore such Cask is best used for Small Beer: The Claret Cask will a great deal sooner be brought into a serviceable State for holding strong Drink, if it is two or three times scalded with Grounds of Barrels, and afterwards used for small Beer for some time. I have bought a Butt or Pipe for eight Shillings in *London* with some Iron Hoops on it, a good Hogshead for the same, and the half Hogshead for five Shillings, the Carriage for a Butt by the Waggon thirty Miles is two Shillings and Sixpence, and the Hogshead Eighteen-pence: But, to cure a Claret Cask of its Colour and Taste, put a Peck of Stone-Lime into a Hogshead, and pour upon it three Pails of Water; bung immediately with a Wood-or Cork Bung, and shake it well about a quarter of an Hour, and let it stand a Day and Night and it will bring off the red Colour, and alter the Taste of the Cask very much. But of three several other excellent Methods for curing musty, stinking, new and other tainted Casks, I have writ of in my Account of Casks in my Second Book.

CHAP. XVIII.

Of Bunging Casks and Carrying of Malt Liquors to some distance.

I am sure this is of no small Consequence, however it may be esteemed as a light matter by some; for if this is not duly perform'd, all our Charge, Labour and Care will be lost; and therefore here I shall dissent from my *London* Fashion, where I bung'd up my Ale with Pots of Clay only, or with Clay mix'd with Bay Salt, which is the better of the two, because this Salt will keep the Clay moist longer than in its Original State; and the Butt Beers and fine Ales were Bung'd with Cork drove in with a piece of Hop-Sack or Rag, which I think are all insipid, and the occasion of spoiling great Quantities of Drink, especially the small Beers; for when the Clay is dry, which is soon in Summer, there cannot be a regular Vent thro' it, and then the Drink from that time flattens and stales to the great loss in a Year to some Owners, and the Benefit of the Brewer; for then a fresh Cask must be Tapp'd to supply it, and the remaining part of the other throw'd away. Now, to prevent this great Inconvenience, my Bung-holes are not quite of the largest size of all, and yet big enough for the common wooden Iron Hoop'd Funnel used in some Brew-houses: In this I put in a turned piece of Ash or Sallow three Inches broad at Top, and two Inches and a half long, first putting in a double piece of dry brown Paper, that is so broad that an Inch or more may be out of it, after the wooden Bung is drove down with a Hammer pretty tight; this Paper must be furl'd or twisted round the Bung, and another loose piece upon and around that, with a little Yeast, and a small Peg put into the Bung, which is to be raised at Discretion when the Beer is drawing, or at other times to give it Vent if there should be occasion: Others will put some Coal or Wood Ashes wetted round this Bung, which will bind very hard, and prevent any Air getting into or out of the Cask; but this in time is apt to rot, and wear the Bung-hole by the Salt or Sulphur in the Ashes, and employing a Knife to scrape it afterwards. Yet, for keeping Beers, it's the best Security of all other ways whatsoever.

There is also a late Invention practised by a common Brewer in the Country that I am acquainted with, for the safe Carriage of Drink on Drays, to some distance without losing any of it, and that is in the Top Center of one of these Bungs, he puts in a wooden Funnel, whose Spout is about four Inches long, and less than half an Inch Diameter at Bottom; this is turned at Top into a concave Fashion like a hollow round Bowl, that will hold about a Pint, which is a constant Vent to the Cask, and yet hinders the Liquor from ascending no faster than the Bowl can receive, and return it again into the Barrel: I may say further, he has brought a Barrel two Miles, and it was then full, when it arrived at his Customers, because the Pint that was put into the Funnel, at setting out, was not at all lost when he took it off the Dray; this may be also made of Tin; and will serve from the Butt to the small Cask.

In the Butt there is a Cork-hole made about two Inches below the upper Head, and close under that a piece of Leather is nailed Spout-fashion, that jetts three Inches out, from which the Yeast works and falls into a Tub, and when the working is over the Cork is put closely in, for the Bung in the Head of the upright

Cask is put in as soon as it is filled up with new Drink: Now when such a Cask is to be broach'd and a quick Draught is to follow, then it may be tapp'd at Bottom; but if otherwise, the Brass Cock ought to be first put in at the middle, and before the Drink sinks to that it should be Tapp'd at Bottom to prevent the breaking of the Head of Yeast, and its growing stale, flat and sour.

In some Places in the Country when they brew Ale or Beer to send to *London* at a great Distance, they let it be a Year old before they Tap it, so that then it is perfectly fine; this they put into small Casks that have a Bung-hole only fit for a large Cork, and then they immediately put in a Role of Bean-flour first kneaded with Water or Drink, and baked in an Oven, which is all secured by pitching in the Cork, and so sent in the Waggon; the Bean-flour feeding and preserving the Body of the Drink all the way, without fretting or causing it to burst the Cask for want of Vent, and when Tapp'd will also make the Drink very brisk, because the Flour is in such a hard Consistence, that it won't dissolve in that time; but if a little does mix with the Ale or Beer, its heavy Parts will sooner fine than thicken the Drink and keep it mellow and lively to the last, if Air is kept out of the Barrel.

CHAP. XIX.

Of the Strength and Age of Malt Liquors.

Whether they be Ales or strong Beers, it is certain that the midling sort is allowed by Physicians to be the most agreeable of any, especially to those of a sedentary Life, or those that are not occupied in such Business as promotes Perspiration enough to throw out and break the Viscidities of the stronger sorts; on which account the laborious Man has the advantage, whose Diet being poor and Body robust, the strength of such Liquors gives a Supply and better digests into Nourishment: But for the unactive Man a Hogshead of Ale which is made from six Bushels of Malt is sufficient for a Diluter of their Food, and will better assist their Constitution than the more strong sort, that would in such produce Obstructions and ill Humours; and therefore that Quantity for Ale, and ten Bushels for a Hogshead of strong Beer that should not be Tapp'd under nine Months, is the most healthful. And this I have experienc'd by enjoying such an Amber Liquor that has been truly brewed from good Malt, as to be of a Vinous Nature, that would permit of a hearty Dose over Night, and yet the next Morning leave a Person light, brisk and unconcern'd. This then is the true Nostrum of Brewing, and ought to be studied and endeavoured for by all those that can afford to follow the foregoing Rules, and then it will supply in a great measure those chargeable (and often adulterated tartarous arthritick) Wines. So likewise for small Beer, especially in a Farmer's Family where it is not of a Body enough, the Drinkers will be feeble in hot Weather and not be able to perform their Work, and will also bring on Distempers, besides the loss of time, and a great waste of such Beer that is generally much thrown away; because Drink is certainly a Nourisher of the Body, as well as Meats, and the more substantial they both are, the better will the Labourer go through his Work, especially at Harvest; and in large Families the Doctor's Bills have proved the Evil of this bad Oeconomy, and far surmounted the Charge of that Malt that would have kept the Servants in good Health, and preserved the Beer from such Waste as the smaller sort is liable to.

'Tis therefore that some prudent Farmers will brew their Ale and small Beer in *March*, by allowing of five or six Bushels of Malt, and two Pounds of Hops to the Hogshead of Ale, and a quarter of Malt and three Pounds of Hops to five Barrels of small Beer. Others there are, that will brew their Ale or strong Beer in *October*, and their small Beer a Month before it is wanted. Others will brew their Ale and small Beer in *April, May* and *June*; but this according to humour, and therefore I have hinted of the several Seasons for Brewing these Liquors: However in my Opinion, whether it be strong or small Drinks, they should be clear, smooth and not too small, if they are design'd for Profit and Health; for if they are otherwise, it will be a sad Evil to Harvest Men, because then they stand most in need of the greatest Balsamicks: To this end some of the softning Ingredients mentioned in the foregoing Receipts should be made use of to feed it accordingly, if these Drinks are brewed forward. And that this particular important Article in the Brewing Oeconomy may be better understood, I shall here recite Dr. *Quincy*'s Opinion of Malt Liquors, viz. The Age of Malt Drinks makes them more or less wholsome, and seems to do somewhat the same as Hops; for those Liquors which are longest kept, are certainly the least viscid; Age by degrees breaking the viscid Parts, and rendering them smaller, makes them finer for Secretion; but this is always to be determined by their Strength, because in Proportion to that will they sooner or later come to their full Perfection and likewise their Decay, until the finer Spirits quite make their Escape, and the remainder becomes vapid and sour. By what therefore has been already said, it will appear that the older Drinks are the more healthful, so they be kept up to this Standard, but not beyond it. Some therefore are of Opinion, that strong Beer brewed in *October* should be Tapp'd at *Midsummer*, and that brewed in *March* at *Christmas*, as being most agreeable to the Seasons of the Year that follow such Brewings: For then they will both have part of a Summer and Winter to ripen and digest their several Bodies; and 'tis my humble Opinion, that where the Strength of the Beer, the Quantity of Hops, the boiling Fermentation and the Cask are all rightly managed, there Drink may be most excellent, and better at nine Months Age, than at nine Years, for Health and Pleasure of Body. But to be truly certain of the right Time, there should be first an Examination made by Pegging the Vessel to prove if such Drink is fine, the Hop sufficiently rotted, and it be mellow and well tasted.

CHAP. XX.

Of the Pleasure and Profit of Private Brewing, and the Charge of buying Malt Liquors.

Here I am to treat of the main Article of shewing the difference between brewing our own Ales and Beers, and buying them, which I doubt not will appear so plain and evident, as to convince any Reader, that many Persons may save well

45

towards half in half, and have their Beer and Ale strong, fine and aged at their own Discretion: A satisfaction that is of no small weight, and the rather since I have now made known a Method of Brewing a Quantity of Malt with a little Copper and a few Tubs, a Secret that has long wanted Publication; for now a Person may Brew in a little Room, and that very safely by keeping his Wort from Foxing, as I have already explained, which by many has been thought impossible heretofore; and this Direction is the more Valuable as there are many Thousands who live in Cities and Towns, that have no more than a few Yards Square of Room to perform a private Brewing in. And as for the trouble, it is easy to account for by those who have time enough on their Hands, and would do nothing else if they had not done this: Or if a Man is paid half a Crown a Day for a Quantity accordingly: Or if a Servant can do this besides his other Work for the same Wages and Charge, I believe the following account will make it appear it is over-ballanc'd considerably, by what such a Person may save in this undertaking, besides the Pleasure of thoroughly knowing the several Ingredients and Cleanliness of the Brewer and Utensils. In several of the Northern Counties of *England*, where they have good Barley, Coak-dryed Malt, and the Drink brewed at Home, there are seldom any bad Ales or Beers, because they have the Knowledge in Brewing so well, that there are hardly any common Brewers amongst them: In the West indeed there are some few, but in the South and East Parts there are many; and now follows the Account, that I have Stated according to my own general Practice, viz.

A Calculation of the Charge and Profit of Brewing six Bushels of Malt for a private Family.

£. s. d.
Six Bushels of Malt at 2s. 8d.
per Bushel, Barley being this)
Year 1733. sold for 14s. *per*) 0 16 0
Quarter by the Farmer)

Hops one Pound 0 1 6

Yeast a Quart 0 0 4

Coals one Bushel, or if Wood or Furze 0 1 0

A Man's Wages a Day 0 2 6

————

Total 1 1 4

Of these six Bushels of Malt I make one Hogshead of Ale and another of Small Beer: But if I was to buy them of some common Brewers, the Charge will be as follows, viz.

£ s. d.

One Hogshead of Ale containing 48)
Gallons, at 6 *d. per* Gallon is) 1 4 0

One Hogshead of Small Beer) containing 54 Gallons, at 2 *d.*) 0 9 0 *per* Gallon

46

is) 0 9 0 ___.___.___
1 13 0 ___.___.___
Total Saved 0 11 8

By the above Account it plainly appears, that 11 s. and 8 d. is clearly gained in Brewing of six Bushels of Malt at our own House for a private Family, and yet I make the Charge fuller by 2 s. and 6 d. then it will happen with many, whose Conveniency by Servants, &c. may intirely take it off; besides the six Bushels of Grains that are currently sold for Three-pence the Bushel, which will make the Eleven and Eight-pence more by four Shillings, without reckoning any thing for yeast, that in the very cheapest time sells here for Four-pence the Quart, and many times there happens three Quarts from so much Drink; so that there may possibly be gained in all sixteen Shillings and Eight-pence: A fine Sum indeed in so small a Quantity of Malt. But here by course will arise a Question, whether this Ale is as good as that bought of some of the common Brewers at Six-pence a Gallon; I can't say all is; however I can aver this, that the Ale I brew in the Country from six Bushels of Malt for my Family, I think is generally full as good, if not better than any I ever sold at that Price in my *London* Brewhouse: And if I should say, that where the Malt, Water and Hops are right good, and the Brewer's Skill answerable to them, there might be a Hogshead of as good Ale and another of small Beer made from five Bushels as I desire to use for my Family, or for Harvest Men; It is no more than I have many times experienced, and 'tis the common length I made for that Purpose. And whoever makes use of true Pale and Amber Malts, and pursues the Directions of this Book, I doubt not but will have their Expectation fully answered in this last Quantity, and so save the great Expence of Excise that the common Brewers Drink is always clogg'd with, which is [blotted text] than five Shillings for Ale and Eighteen-pence *per* Barrel for Small Beer.

CHAP. XXI.

A Philosophical Account for Brewing strong October *Beer. By an Ingenious Hand.*

In Brewing, your Malt ought to be sound and good, and after its making to lye two or more Months in the Heap, to come to such a temper, that the Kernel may readily melt in the washing.

The well dressing your Malt, ought to be one chief Care; for unless it be freed from the Tails and Dust, your Drink will not be fine and mellow as when it is clean dressed.

The grinding also must be considered according to the high or low drying of the Malt; for if high dryed, then a gross grinding is best, otherwise a smaller may be done; for the Care in grinding consists herein, lest too much of the Husk being ground small should mix with the Liquor, which makes a gross Feces, and consequently your Drink will have too fierce a Fermentation, and by that means make it Acid, or that we call Stale.

When your Malt is ground, let it stand in Sacks twenty-four Hours at least, to the end that the Heat in grinding may be allayed, and 'tis conceived by its so standing that the Kernel will dissolve the better.

The measure and quantity we allow of Hops and Malt, is five Quarter of Malt to three Hogsheads of Beer, and eighteen Pounds of Hops at least to that Quantity of Malt, and if Malt be pale dryed, then add three or four Pounds of Hops more.

The Choice of Liquor for Brewing is of considerable advantage in making good Drink, the softest and cleanest water is to be prererr'd, your harsh water is not to be made use of.

You are to boil your first Liquor, adding a Handful or two of Hops to it, then before you strike it over to your Goods or Malt, cool in as much Liquor, as will bring it to a temper not to scald the Malt, for it is a fault not to take the Liquor as high as possible but not to scald. The next Liquors do the same.

And indeed all your Liquors ought to be taken as high as may be, that is not to scald.

When you let your Wort from your Malt into the Underback, put to it a Handful or two of Hops, 'twill preserve it from that accident which Brewers call Blinking or Foxing.

In boiling your Worts, the first Wort boil high or quick; for the quicker the first Wort is boiled, the better it is.

The second boil more than the first, and the third or last more than the second.

In cooling lay your Worts thin, and let each be well cooled, and Care must be taken in letting them down into the Tun, that you do it leisurely, to the end that as little of the Feces or Sediment which causes the Fermentation to be fierce or mild, for Note, there is in all fermented Liquors, Salt and Sulphur, and to keep these two Bodies in a due Proportion, that the Salt does not exalt itself above the Sulphur, consists a great part of the Art in Brewing.

When your Wort is first let into your Tun, put but a little Yeast to it, and let it work by degrees quietly, and if you find it works but moderate, whip in the Yeast two or three times or more, till you find your Drink well fermented, for without a full opening of the Body by fermentation, it will not be perfect fine, nor will it drink clean and light.

When you cleanse, do it by a Cock from your Tun, placed six Inches from the Bottom, to the end that most of the Sediment may be left behind, which may be thrown on your Malt to mend your Small Beer.

When your Drink is Tunn'd, fill your Vessel full, let it work at the Bung-hole, and have a reserve in a small Cask to fill it up, and don't put any of the Drink which will be under the Yeast after it is work'd over into your Vessels, but put it by itself in another Cask, for it will not be so good as your other in the Cask.

This done, you must wait for the finishing of the fermentation, then stop it close, and let it stand till the Spring, for Brewing ought to be done in the Month of *October*, that it may have time to settle and digest all the Winter Season.

In the Spring you must unstop your Vent-hole and thereby see whether your Drink doth ferment or not, for as soon as the warm Weather comes, your Drink will have another fermentation, which when it is over, let it be again well stopped and stand till *September* or longer, and then Peg it; and if you find it pretty fine, the Hop well rotted and of a good pleasant taste for drinking.

Then and not before draw out a Gallon of it, put to it two Ounces of Ising-glass cut small and well beaten to melt, stirring it often and whip it with a Wisk till the Ising-glass be melted, then strain it and put it into your Vessel, stirring it well together, stop the Bung slightly, for this will cause a new and small fermentation, when that is over stop it close, leaving only a Vent-hole a little stopp'd, let it stand, and in ten Days or a little more, it will be transparently fine, and you may drink of it out of the Vessel till two parts in three be drawn, then Bottle the rest, which will in a little time come to drink very well. If your Drink in *September* be well condition'd for taste, but not fine, and you desire to drink it presently, rack it before you put your Ising-glass to it, and then it will fine the better and drink the cleaner.

To make Drink fine quickly, I have been told that by separating the Liquor from the Feces, when the Wort is let out of the Tun into the Underback, which may be done in this manner, when you let your Wort into your Underback out of your Tun, catch the Wort in some Tub so long, and so often as you find it run foul, put that so catched on the Malt again, and do so till the Wort run clear into the Underback. This is to me a very good way (where it may be done) for 'tis the Feces which causes the fierce and violent fermentation, and to hinder that in some measure is the way to have fine Drink: Note that the finer you make your Wort, the sooner your Drink will be fine, for I have heard that some Curious in Brewing have caused Flannels to be so placed, that all the Wort may run thro' one or more of them into the Tun before working, by which means the Drink was made very fine and well tasted.

Observations on the foregoing Account.

This Excellent Philosophical Account of Brewing *October* Beer, has hitherto remained in private Hands as a very great Secret, and was given to a Friend of mine by the Author himself, to whom the World is much obliged, altho' it comes by me; In justice therefore to this ingenious Person, I would here mention his Name, had I leave for so doing; but at present this Intimation must suffice. However, I shall here take notice, that his Caution against using tailed or dusty Malt, which is too commonly sold, is truly worthy of Observation; for these are so far from producing more Ale or Beer, that they absorb and drink part of it up.

In Grinding Malts he notifies well to prevent a foul Drink.

The quantity he allows is something above thirteen Bushels to the Hogshead which is very sufficient; but this as every body pleases.

The Choice of Liquors or Waters for Brewing, he says, is of considerable advantage; and so must every body else that knows their Natures and loves Health, and pleasant Drink: For this purpose, in my Opinion, the Air and Soil is to be regarded where the Brewing is performed; since the Air affects all things it can come at, whether Animal, Vegetable or Mineral, as may be proved from many Instances: In the Marshes of *Kent* and *Essex*, the Air there is generally so infectious by means of those low vaesy boggy Grounds, that seldom a Person escapes an Ague one time or other, whether Natives or Aliens, and is often fatally known to some of the *Londoners* and others who merrily and nimbly travel down to the Isles of *Grain* and *Sheppy* for a valuable Harvest, but in a Month's time they generally return thro' the Village of *Soorne* with another Mien. There is also a little *Moor* in *Hertfordshire*, thro' which a Water runs that frequently gives the *Passant* Horses that drink of it, the Colick or Gripes, by means of the aluminous sharp Particles of its Earth; Its Air is also so bad, as has obliged several to remove from its Situation for their Healths: The Dominion of the Air is likewise so powerful over Vegetables, that what will grow in one Place won't in another, as is plain from the Beech and Black Cherry Tree, that refuse the Vale of *Ailesbury* tho' on some Hills there, yet will thrive in the *Chiltern* or Hilly Country: So the Limes and other Trees about *London* are all generally black-barked, while those in the Country are most of them of a Silver white. Water is also so far under the Influence of the Air and Soil, as makes many excellent for Brewing when others are as bad. In Rivers, that run thro' boggy Places, the Sullage or Washings of such Soils are generally unwholsome as the nature of such Ground is; and so the Water becomes infected by that and the Effluvia or Vapour that accompanies such Water: So Ponds are surely good or bad, as they are under too much Cover or supply'd by nasty Drains, or as they stand situated or exposed to good and bad Airs. Thus the Well-waters by consequence share in the good or bad Effects of such Soils that they run thorough, and the very Surface of the Earth by which such Waters are strained, is surely endowed with the quality of the Air in which it lies; which brings me to my intended purpose, to prove that Water drawn out of a Chalky, or Fire-stone Well, which is situated under a dry sweet loamy Soil, in a fine pure Air, and that is perfectly soft, must excel most if not all other Well-waters for the purpose in Brewing. The Worts also that are rooted in such an Air, in course partakes of its nitrous Benefits, as being much exposed thereto in the high Backs or Coolers that contain them. In my own Grounds I have Chalks under Clays and Loams; but as the latter is better than the former, so the Water proves more soft and wholsome under one than the other. Hence then may be observed the contrary Quality of those harsh curdling Well-waters that many drink of in their Malt Liquors, without considering their ill Effects, which are justly condemn'd by this able Author as unfit to be made use of in Brewing *October* Beer.

The boiling a few Hops in the first Water is good, but they must be strained thro' a Sieve before the Water is put into the Malt; and to check its Heat with cold Liquor, or to let it stand to cool some time, is a right Method, lest it scalds and locks up the Pores of the Malt, which would then yield a thick Wort to the end of the Brewing and never be good Drink.

His putting Hops into the Underback, is an excellent Contrivance to prevent foxing, as I have already hinted.

The quick boiling of the Wort is of no less Service, and that the smaller Wort should be boiled longer than the strong is good Judgment, because the stronger the Wort, the sooner the Spirits flie away and the waste of more Consequence; besides if the first Wort was to be boiled too long, it would obtain so thick a Body, as to prevent in great measure its fining hereafter after so soon in the Barrel; while the smaller sort will evaporate its more watry Parts, and thereby be brought into a thicker Confidence, which is perfectly necessary in thin Worts; and in this Article lies so much the Skill of the Brewer, that some will make a longer Length than ordinary from the Goods for Small Beer, to shorten it afterwards in the Copper by Length of boiling, and this way of consuming it is the more natural, because the remaining part will be better Cured.

The laying Worts thin is a most necessary Precaution; for this is one way to prevent their running into Cohesions and Foxing, the want of which Knowledge and Care has undoubtedly been the occasion of great Losses in Brewing; for when Worts are tainted in any considerable degree, they will be ropy in time and unfit for the human Body, as being unwholsome as well as unpleasant. So likewise is his *Item* of great Importance, when he advises to draw the Worts off fine out of the Backs or Coolers, and leave the Feces or Sediments behind, by reason, as he says, they are the cause of those two detested Qualities in Malt Liquors, staleness and foulness, two Properties that ought to imploy the greatest Care in Brewers to prevent; for 'tis certain these Sediments are a Composition of the very worst part of the Malt, Hops and Yeast, and, while they are in the Barrel, will so tincture and impregnate the Drink with their insanous and unpleasant nature, that its Drinkers will be sure to participate thereof more or less as they have lain together a longer or a shorter time. To have then a Malt Drink balsamick and mild, the Worts cannot be run off too fine from the Coolers, nor well fermented too slow, that there may be a Medium kept, in both the Salt and Sulphur that all fermented Malt Drinks abound with, and herein, as he says, lies a great part of the Art of Brewing.

He says truly well, that a little Yeast at first should be put to the Wort, that it may quietly work by degrees, and not be violently forc'd into a high Fermentation; for then by course the Salt and Sulphur will be too violently agitated into such an Excess and Disagreement of Parts, that will break their Unity into irregular Commotions, and cause the Drink to be soon stale and harsh. But if it should be too backward and work too moderate, then whipping the Yeast two or three times into it will be of some service to open the Body of the Beer, for as he observes, if Drink has not a due fermentation, it will not be fine, clean, nor light.

His advice to draw the Drink out of the Tun by a Cock at such a distance from the bottom is right; because that room will best keep the Feces from being disturb'd as the Drink is drawing off, and leaving them behind; but for putting them afterwards over the Malt for Small Beer, I don't hold it consonant with good Brewing, by reason in this Sediment there are many Particles of the Yeast, that consequently will cause a small Fermentation in the Liquor and Malt, and be a means to spoil rather than make good Small Beer.

What he says of filling up the Cask with a reserve of the same Drink, and not with that which has once worked out, is past dispute just and right.

And so is what he says of stopping up the Vessel close after the Fermentation is over; but that it is best to Brew all strong Beer in *October*, I must here take leave to dissent from the Tenet, because there is room for several Objections in relation to the sort of Malt and Cellar, which as I have before explained, shall say the less here.

As he observes Care should be taken in the Spring to unstop the Vent, lest the warm Weather cause such a Fermentation as may burst the Cask, and also in *September*, that it be first try'd by Pegging if the Drink is fine, well tasted and the Hop rotted; and then if his Way is liked best, bring the rest into a transparent Fineness; for Clearness in Malt Liquors, as I said before, and here repeat it again, is a most agreeable Quality that every Man ought to enjoy for his Health and Pleasure, and therefore he advises for dispatch in this Affair, and to have the Drink very fine, to rack it off before the Ising-glass is put in; but I can't be a Votary for this Practice, as believing the Drink must lose a great deal of its Spirits by such shifting; yet I must chime in with his Notion of putting the Wort so often over the Malt till it comes off fine as I have already taught, which is a Method that has been used many Years in the North of *England*, where they are so curious as to let the Wort lie some time in the Underback to draw it off from the Feces there; nor are they less careful to run it fine out of the Cooler into the Tun, and from that into the Cask; in all which three several Places the Wort and Drink may be had clear and fine, and then there will be no more Sediments than is just necessary to assist and seed the Beer, and preserving its Spirits in a due Temper. But if Persons have Time and Conveniency, and their Inclination leads them to, obtain their Drink in the utmost Fineness, it is an extraordinary good way to use *Hippocrates* Sleeve or Flannel Bag, which I did in my great Brew-house at *London* for straining off the Feces that were left in the Backs. As to the Quantity of Malt for Brewing a Hogshead of *October* Beer, I am of Opinion thirteen Bushels are right, and so are ten, fifteen and twenty, according as People approve of; for near *Litchfield*, I know some have brewed a Hogshead of *October* Beer from sixteen Bushels of Barley Malt, one of Wheat, one of Beans, one of Pease and one of Oat Malt, besides hanging a Bag of Flower taken out of the last four Malts in the Hogshead for the Drink to feed on, nor can a certain Time Be limited and adjusted for the Tapping of any Drink (notwithstanding what has been affirmed to the contrary) because some Hops will not be rotted so soon as others, and some Drinks will not fine so soon as others; as is evident in the Pale Malt Drinks, that will seldom or never break so soon in the Copper as the Brown sort, nor will they be so soon ripe and fit to Tap as the high dryed Malt Drink will. Therefore what this Gentleman says of trying Drink by first Pegging it before it is Tapp'd, in my Opinion is more just and right than relying on a limited time for Broaching such Beer.

Printed in Great Britain
by Amazon.co.uk, Ltd.,
Marston Gate.